Old Boy

Georgia Tree was born in Subiaco, Western Australia, in 1992. She's since spent most of her life by the ocean – first Dampier in the Pilbara, and later Warnbro in the deep south outer suburbs of Perth. Georgia studied Creative Writing at Curtin University, graduating with Honours in 2013, and in 2020 she completed a Master of International Relations and National Security. Georgia now works as a Senior Adviser in the Albanese Labor Government and lives in Mount Lawley with her hairless cat, Princess Margarita.

Old Boy

GEORGIA TREE

Published with support from the
Dorothy and Bill Irwin Charitable Trust.

For Jocelyn, my grandmother,

and

for Callan, my favourite

CONTENTS

REWIND

Dad pushes against the flywire with his shoulder, his arm bracing two mugs of black coffee. The flywire – now banging open against the bricks – is shredded from years of weather damage and scratches from the dogs that lived here before Trevor moved in. I sit in a patch of shade on the faded rattan couch that's been here as long as I can remember, next to Trevor, who is sprawled out in the sun. Dad sets the mugs on the dusty table he built himself and drags a packet of Winfield Golds out of the back pocket of his jeans.

Dad's house is wedged between the main road and the primary school. Across the road is the park where we'd jump off our bikes and walk them across to stop the magpies swooping at our helmets. Walk a couple of minutes towards the beach, and you'll find Nan's old house – salty and bore-water stained – where my oldest cousin taught me how to rain dance. It's right by the Warnbro Tavern that now goes by another name where Mum last worked before moving up north to meet Dad.

Dad's backyard is overgrown and too green for summer. The old eucalyptus tree that used to shade the side of the house has been reduced to a pile of mulch. Every day he carts a wheelbarrow full of it, taking it from the side of the house to the front lawn. Wheelbarrow tracks are two wet lines which run over the brick paving he did himself when we moved in. It's still intact, save for a sinkhole under the gutter pipe next to the barbecue. I've come from the hairdresser's down the road and my head tingles where the bleach has burnt the psoriasis off. The faintest breeze blows Trevor's ginger fur into the air, and the window of sunlight throws the strands into relief. They look almost still – suspended, midair.

A willie wagtail sits black against the red of the bottlebrush by the car port. Its nest is falling apart. I can hear kids in the cricket nets across the road at the park, where Dad broke his finger playing footy with my brother and ended up in Freo Hospital with a screw in his hand, down a couple of levels from Mum – inpatient at the oncology ward.

There are bushfires on the East Coast. The government refuses to draw a link between the destruction and a changing climate. Volunteer firefighters refuse to shake the Prime Minister's hand.

But it's quiet here for now.

I get my phone out of my bag and pull up the voice-recording app with the flick of a thumb, like I do at press conferences or for radio or TV interviews. All the files are there, saved automatically under the location of the recording. Parliament House 11, Parliament House 10, Parliament House 7, Sky News. All with little grey date stamps in the margins. I tap the red button on the screen and prop my phone up against the marble ashtray on the dusty table.

Dad looks nervous. My whole life he's been telling me that I'll be the one to write his story. Maybe he already knows he will talk for days that stretch on for months. He will say things he'd never even thought before, let alone said out loud. As he goes on talking, the world will change. We'll all be plunged into hibernation. Isolation. Equitably vulnerable. With nowhere to look but inside. He probably knew even then – that by the end of it all – it still won't make sense why he lived. That there's no reason, other than that life is grotesque. Dying can be a game of chance as much as flipping a coin or winning a footy game. And living can be a choice too.

I'll spend hours interviewing Dad, months scouring transcripts. I'll drive through each street, and pull over and stop at the houses where I know he lived. I'll waste time on Cottesloe Beach. I'll pore over the history of this place – our home. I'll ride my bike around Rottnest Island. I'll fly to the Pilbara and back. I'll learn the story of Charlie – the boy from the other side of the river – and feel compelled to tell his story too. I'll piece together the fragments of Dad's memory – the fallible recollections, the malleable truths. And I'll bridge the gaps in his memory to shape the narrative of his story – the beginning of mine.

But right now, I want to put him out of his misery. Offer to do it another time. But I don't. Instead, I sit here on the couch with the cat and the afternoon sun creeping onto my face, drag a Winfield Gold out of the packet resting on the table, and begin.

To get to know the Old Boy.

ON PAROLE

Peter necked his pint.

'Are you right to drive, Grant?' he asked, chucking me the keys.

I wasn't drunk. But I still didn't have my licence back. In fact, I thought there was a letter back at Mum and Dave's about an appointment at the licensing centre for the next week. If I got caught again it'd be another six months. I was still on parole.

'Yeah, no worries,' I said.

It'd been raining, but it was that time of year where it was just starting to get warmer and the air smelled like school holidays. Royal Show weather.

Stirling Highway was quiet and getting dark. Everyone must've been at the game. Peter lit a cigarette and rolled down the window. I turned on the radio.

With two minutes left of the third term, the Tigers had managed just one minor score after half-time.

'Swans are killing us,' said Peter.

I pulled into the right lane but there was a car, and I swerved left just as the road bent at Wellington. I corrected but it was too late, and I collected the footpath and my foot was flat on the brake and my head whipped forward as the car was stopped by a lamppost. I couldn't feel anything. I looked over at Peter. His body was limp, head face down on the dash. I ripped the car door open and ran to a house where a lady was opening the front door. We weren't far from Mum and Dave's.

'Quick, get an ambulance,' I think I said.

The lady ran inside. I looked at the car and at Peter limp over the dash. I imagined blood pouring down his face. I imagined I heard sirens. I felt a hot trickle down the back of my neck and tasted metal in my mouth.

And I ran.

I didn't know where I was running except away from the highway. I thought I was running to the river, but I was still not sure what side of the road we'd been driving on. I didn't know where I was running until I was banging on the front door. Charlie's place. Susie answered the door.

'What's happened?' Susie asked, steering me inside.

It smelled like Sunday roast. The leather couch felt cool against my back.

'It's clearly an accident, mate. It'll be okay,' said Charlie.

'I don't want to go back inside,' I said.

Susie nursed me like one of her Graylands patients, patting my forehead with a damp flannel. Charlie lit me a cigarette.

'Your old man is a copper, isn't he? He'll be able to help.'

'You don't know my old man.'

Susie lightly ran her hand along my shoulders, left to right. The touch of her hand tracing lines across my back was all I could feel in my entire body. I held on to that.

'Is he home?' Charlie asked, patting his keys in his pocket.

'No, they'll be at the footy club.'

'Hope he's not a Tigers fan.'

'He is.'

Charlie laughed, and picked up the cream telephone with the long cord from the desk, carrying it over to the table beside me.

'Well then, he's already had a shit day anyway. Give him a call.'

I called the Claremont Footy Club and asked for my stepfather and Dave came and picked me up. He came without Mum. I didn't say anything as we drove to the Claremont Police Station, but Dave talked at me – telling me what to say, telling me what not to say. He didn't want me to go back inside either.

'You won't be getting your bloody licence back anytime

soon!' he said as we pulled into the car park, the familiar chequered blue sign waiting for us.

I thought he was enjoying it. It must have been a shocking game. I was glad I called him.

I've returned to that place in my mind too many times to count. The cream phone. Charlie's laugh. Susie's hand on my back.

Within a year Susie would die in a car accident herself, and Charlie would be on death row.

But I didn't know that then. That night they really saved my skin.

PART ONE

1963–1975

LYALL STREET

There was no shade in the car park out the front of the Swanbourne Hotel. We had the windows rolled down but it was still hot in the car. It was one of those days where it hurts to look at the sun. The Norfolk pine on the right flank was just like every other around here, but the palm trees in the beer garden and the art deco architecture made it look like someplace else. I could have probably gone in if Pippin and Scott weren't in the car. We'd already finished our fire engine when Pippin passed me the packet of salt and vinegar chips, and I heard the shouting before I saw them. Mum and Dad. On the front steps, right in the middle of the palm trees. Scott started crying then. Pippin shushed him, cradling him like he was her own little baby. A toy doll. She was only four. Then Mum got in the car without Dad and started driving the wrong way. We were past the cemetery when she said,

'We're going to Ga's house.' Pippin didn't say anything, but I could tell she was worried because she left her doll at Rob Roy Street. My footy was there too.

I'd had a dream the night before, at Rob Roy Street. A nightmare, really. There were all these little people – little gremlins – lifting up my bed. I woke up so scared.

I do remember my parents being happy sometimes. I think they were happy when we went to watch Dad play cricket and he had a win, and we'd spend all night at the WACA, Scott, Pippin and I – running up and down the wooden stairs in the grandstand, playing with the frogs in the gutter, while Mum and Dad sat at the bar and sang and drank. Back when they kept a flock of sheep at the ground to keep the grass down. But I mostly remember them arguing.

It felt like it took a long time to get to our grandparents' house on Lyall Street in Shenton Park. Scott never stopped crying. We were barely in the door before Mum was back out again, climbing into the car. She told Ga she was moving to Port Hedland for work. We wouldn't see her again until Christmas. I was about six.

It was quieter at Ga's place. The little house on Lyall Street was surrounded by a white picket fence and protected by the shade of the giant Moreton Bay figs, with their gnarled and crooked trunks, which lined the quiet street. Across the road was a big wooden fence which enclosed the backyards of the houses parallel. Brown leaves littered the footpaths. Ga was, on the face of it, like any other grandmother. She spent her time knitting and crocheting, cooking and cleaning, and having people over for tea. She was stoic. The quintessential Australian matriarch, despite her being a ten-pound Pom. Jempa worked shiftwork, stereotyping at the *West Australian* in town, running maintenance for the mechanical printing machines for the newspaper. He loved his sport, Jempa. He'd scored a tryout with Tottenham Hotspur Football Club back in England, but he never made it. He got on a boat to Australia instead. If Jempa wasn't at work, he was at the pub. He rode his bike in to work every day because he was still scared of vehicles from the war. I think it was a motorbike accident he had. He wouldn't even ride the train.

We got around on our bikes too, mostly. Perth was still under construction then. Everywhere you went, there were big piles of yellow sand. At the hospital site we'd dig trenches and build bases – cover for the boondie fights. Boondie warfare was rampant, with every yellow sand pile a theatre of war. Along the railway line there were train stations half complete, unfenced, with sand gullies flanking the platforms, just asking to be exploited. They offered perfect cover. When the trains were full at Royal Show time, Scott and I would crouch in our sand trenches, waiting for the train to arrive, then start to move off again – packed with people – before peppering the carriage with jumping jack crackers through the open windows. We'd laugh so loud it almost drowned out the screams.

I started playing footy around then. At the Subiaco Police and Citizens footy club. Although I spent a lot of time on the bench. Ga probably just wanted us out of the house.

I still dream about Lyall Street. I suppose that's the same for most people. Like the place you first started forming memories is the foundation for your own subconscious, or something like that. The street still looks the same too, with the big old Moreton Bay figs. Ga and Jempa's place was knocked down in the nineties, though.

***

We were starting to get bored. Peter, my friend from Rosalie Primary, had already gone home – but Scott and I were carrying on, crouching in our makeshift cubby under the bridge near the Shenton Park train station, sparring.

'Hey, that hurt!' Scott yelled as my stick bent against his elbow. You could see the little white holes where it punctured the skin, but no blood yet.

'Okay, let's go then.'

I rubbed and clapped my hands together, but I couldn't

get rid of all the sand. It felt like it was glued to my skin. We walked along the railway line towards home. I looked over my shoulder at the train parked up at the platform. It was closing its doors, with people spilling out onto the pavement. Men in suits with briefcases were pushing their way out of the carriages. I imagined Dad was one of them. The train whistled and sounded its horn. And again. And again. It was an alarming sound. But I didn't understand. We were on the other track.

'Grant!'

Scott was on the other side of the track by the road, his face white, pointing ahead at the train coming from the city end. Hurtling towards me. I dived into the middle of the tracks and braced myself. The screeching and crunching of metal flooded everything until it stopped. I could feel both trains had passed but it took a little minute to stand up and jump back over the road side to Scott.

You wouldn't believe the look on his face.

'Just don't say anything to Ga,' I said.

'I thought you died!'

'Well I didn't. But if you tell Ga she'll murder us both.' I looked at Scott with a warning which he well understood. The last thing we needed was a belting.

I was always the one copping a belting. Probably because I was the eldest. And I was always getting into trouble.

I didn't mind Ga's beltings really, they were mechanical – a rap over knuckles with Jempa's belt buckle or a slap on the bum with the wooden spoon. It was Jempa coming home after a night at the pub that worried me.

Ga and Pippin were in the kitchen when we made it home. Jempa was on the couch, a king brown of Swan Gold in hand. We went straight to the bathroom to wash away the blood and the sand before anyone got a good look at us. Pippin was finishing up setting the table when we sat down for tea. She looked at us both like she knew all of our sins, pursing her lips but saying nothing. Ga served up the roast – chicken. Jempa didn't come. Instead he lay on the couch, occasionally popping in to grab another KB out of the fridge. That wasn't unusual. And I didn't mind. There was a different energy when he was in the room. Tense. Like a stray cat.

***

I didn't mind Rosalie Primary. The boys from class would muck around with Scott and me. So much so that days spent in school and outside on our bikes and in the sand blend together in my memory. We didn't have a TV at Rosalie so, in my final year of primary school, when the morning edition of the *West Australian* had printed details on the front page of how to watch American astronauts land on the moon for the first time, the class was in a panic. We had a TV at home, of course, but the moon landing was in two hours time. Ga would kill me if I missed school. And Jempa would be home.

'Miss, we have to watch the moon landing. It's historic,' Peter said as soon as Miss Thompson walked through the classroom door.

Peter was my best friend. He seemed to know a lot about the world. He was confident too. And always talking about his dad.

Peter had the paper strewn across a pentagon of desks by the blackboard up front, us students – aspiring astronauts and adventurers – gathered around it.

'We'll have to listen to the wireless, Peter,' she said, already defeated.

'No, Miss, we have to watch it. Surely they have a TV at Hollywood High?'

'I'm sure they do, but we can't get there.'

Peter looked mutinous. I could feel heat creeping up the back of my neck. Peter knew that I had a TV at home. It wasn't as far as Hollywood either. Peter's eyes swept the class, looking us over, desperate for someone to give. Then Gilbert wandered in. He lived right across the road from school, on Yilgarn Street, and he was always running late. Peter's eyes lit up.

'Gilbert, does your old man have a TV?'

'Yes.'

Peter looked at Miss Thompson, who didn't have it in her to put up a fight. It didn't take long to herd the class across the road and into Gilbert's front room. Peter and I sat on the ground behind the glass-topped coffee table, cross-legged, our arms folded on the glass. Miss Thompson sat on the arm of the couch, smoking, tapping the ash into an ashtray resting on her thigh. The black-and-white TV was snowy as hell, and the voices of the men off-screen garbled and alien. But nobody spoke, we just sat and watched. Big, bold numbers ticked down by the second to single digits. The garbled voices continued speaking numbers and altitude interlaced with long beeps until the TV screen filled with the milky white of the moon's surface. The shuttle landing on the moon looked like a meteor burning towards earth.

'The *Eagle* is in Tranquility,' a man on the TV said.

Peter looked at me then, in shock, I think. I felt a dead weight on my chest and a lump in my throat. Miss Thompson crushed her cigarette, placing the ashtray on the coffee table as she stood.

'That's it, kids. The *Eagle* has landed. Let's go.'

I don't know if it had that feeling that each shared, momentous event has on the human psyche – of togetherness and witnessing history in action – or if it was just fun to get out of class. But I remember that feeling in my stomach watching the spacecraft make contact with the moon, the collective gasp of air of all of us and the smell of Miss Thompson's cigarette smoke.

That night Jempa was late home. The train drivers were on strike, he said. I was unsure how that affected him, given he rode his bike and never took the train anyway. But he used the opportunity to explain to me what a union was.

'They're trying to get a rise in their wages. They're playing hardball,' he said. 'The government are trying to weasel out of it because of inflation, they reckon.'

I nodded along. I didn't understand what inflation meant, but I got the general gist of these guys wanting more money for their work.

'Will they win? The train drivers?' I asked.

'I hope so,' said Jempa.

It was not long after that Mum came home for good. She was sitting there at Ga's table with a cup of tea in one hand and baby in the other. Pippin stood over her shoulder, hands clasped together, eyes on her baby sister. Ga watched her daughter, but her hands never stopped knitting – this time a romper for the baby.

'You'll be moving in with us in Mosman Park,' Mum said, her eyes moving from me, to Pippin, to Scott, to the baby. She'd had a bit of sun in Port Hedland and she looked a little older. Ga told us she'd got married. Mum still had long, blonde hair, set in waves, pinned up on her head. And she wore a shocking pink dress with a high neck and circle skirt.

'We've already enrolled you at Swanbourne High, Grant. And Pippin will be there the following year.'

'But I want to go to Hollywood.'

Mum looked at me. She looked tired. 'Why?'

'All my friends will be there.'

Mum looked at Ga, who said nothing with her mouth.

'Well, you'll be catching the train there. Don't expect me to drive you.'

I nodded, banking the victory. Pippin and Scott said nothing.

Would she have come home at all if Ga hadn't been diagnosed with breast cancer?

The baby started to cry.

Back then, Hollywood High was the biggest public school in the richest area of Perth. Sandwiched right between the hospital and the cemetery. It felt like everyone who was anyone was going there, in the seventies anyway. It's since been knocked down – the prime real estate repurposed into expensive townhouses and apartment blocks. Occasionally I drive through the streets on the way to a funeral or something and forget that it was ever there. There's just no trace of it.

But in 1970, Hollywood High was full of ratbags, me included. I was really little then; you wouldn't believe it now. But I got on with the other short guys around. We were always starting fights at lunch, us three little guys. Fights that we rarely finished. Most of my cousins were at Hollywood too. As well as my footy mates from Mosman Park, like Gary, Johnny, Michael and Brett. There were a lot of British migrants – skinheads. All sorts. The skinheads were alright to smoke with but we got into a lot of fights. I don't remember learning much, though.

I still took Scott with me everywhere. Mostly because Mum and Dave wouldn't let him go anywhere without me. Dave – Mum's new husband – was a copper. They got together while he was stationed in Port Hedland. But they actually met years earlier, when he went around to our house – as a rookie cop – to pick up Mum's expired rego plates for her Morris Minor. And then again at Rottnest a couple of times. When he was much thinner, according to Mum. He was alright, I supposed. But he was hard on me, to prove a point. I took Scott along with me to the speedway every Friday night, for example. Scott bloody loved the speedway. We'd get on the train at Grant Street to the Claremont Showgrounds together. Perched low on the grass hill, close enough to the fence that you could smell the tar, watching the cars chase and circle round. Engines roared. It was so loud at times we had to cover our ears.

'Can we go closer?' Scott yelled one time, motioning towards the fence, hanging tired with the weight of boys lined up along it, their fingers poking through the wire holes. We joined them against the fence, the roaring so loud that I couldn't hear Scott screaming. A car skidded out in front of us, flicking up huge chunks of dirt and sand in its wake, showering us and the other boys on the fence. I looked over at Scott. I could see he was crying, clutching at his eye.

Mum ripped me a new one when we got home.

'What is wrong with you, Grant? Why did you have to get so close?' Mum snapped at me, pulling bandages and bottles of ointment and Betadine out of the medicine box. Scott was seated at the table, his head back. Dave was standing over him, eye drops in hand. Every now and then he'd put a couple of droplets of liquid into Scott's eye, and Scott would squeal in response.

'I'm sorry,' I said.

Pippin was sitting on the stairs with baby Jodee and Jodee's dollies in her lap, Mr Christian – the golden labrador – curled up under their feet.

'What is wrong with you?' Mum said again.

I'm sure I didn't know.

THE OLD POLICE STATION ON STIRLING HIGHWAY

'Now, bloke, don't let Mr Christian out. He'll get hit by a car out there.'

Dave always looked more intimidating when he had his police uniform on. God knows why it was my responsibility to look after the dog. If he did get out, it wouldn't be long until the news got back to Dave at Cottesloe Police Station. He wouldn't be inconspicuous either – a great big golden lab trotting down Stirling Highway. And I had plans to surf, so I decided to take Mr Christian with me. The old blokes at the pub could keep an eye on him.

The water cooled my feet, burnt from the sand and the road. There were a few other grommets out but I didn't recognise any of them. Swell was about three metres.

My foam Coolite felt light under me as I paddled hard for the first wave. I didn't time it right. I turned around, paddling back out, waiting for a wave big enough to carry me. I felt a wave coming and paddled faster this time, jumping up quick as it propelled me forward. Too fast. Too much weight on one side. I tumbled over the board, face first. Salt water poured into my mouth and lungs and out of my nose. I smelt coconut wax. I climbed back on and paddled back out. As soon as I felt the wave build under me, I knew I'd already missed it but I paddled as hard as I could anyway. To my right and just in front a kid was paddling for the same wave. At the same moment I felt the wave pass me, it projected him forward, the kid rising to his feet and riding it for what must have felt like an eternity to the shore. When he paddled back to the spot, he was smiling.

I recognised him from footy now, a young Aboriginal kid from Christ Church Grammar – Sam. He was on a single-fin shortboard. I decided I was done with the Coolite.

Sam and I found Christian at the Cott Hotel with the old blokes. The Cottesloe Hotel looked then like it does now, a white art-deco structure with the curved corner piece overlooking the beach front. Swan Draught on tap. Regulars at the counter. Footy on the TV.

Pope was holding court at the front bar.

'Yeah, and that Kevin Murray, I wouldn't hesitate to knock him out again,' Pope said.

'The footballer?' asked Sam, eyes wide.

'Yeah, I don't give a shit how many Brownlows he has, you don't play up at the pub.'

The old blokes roared with laughter. Pope had Mr Christian under his feet, little drops of condensation from his pint dripping down onto the dog's head.

'Have I ever told you boys about the clock?'

Pope was a real character. He was a war veteran, but in a different way from Jempa. He wasn't broken.

I'd heard this particular Pope story before but I knew Sam hadn't, so I let it go.

'You see that clock up there?' said Pope, pointing up at the west-facing wall, above the windows, at a giant cream-faced clock with brass hands and roman numerals.

'Yep,' said Sam.

'Well, that clock's been there since the Second World War. The pub's changed hands a few times, but that clock hasn't moved.'

'*Hadn't* moved,' barked one of the old blokes, met with snorts of agreement.

'But when this bloke came in,' Pope said, his thumb pointing behind him, towards the kitchen, 'he wants to redecorate the place. And we hear he's going to get rid of the clock.'

Sam looked up at the clock again. Still obviously there.

'So we weren't having that. We took it for safekeeping before he could flog it off.'

'I was down the pub the next day and everyone was saying, "Someone's knocked off the clock!"' Brickhead – Pope's son – started.

'So I get to the old man's place to tell him and he's got this bloody grin on his face. He's put the clock up on the wall!'

The old blokes and Sam and I roared.

'I brought it back!' said Pope, grinning. 'I don't even really like the clock. It's the principle of the thing.'

My feet were blistered when I got home to the old police station where we lived on Stirling Highway. My eyes stinging from the spray of the ocean and the glare of the sun. Mouth dry from the pints. Mr Christian sat under my feet, his belly rising and falling in time with his breath. Dave came home late that night, but he walked straight up the stairs to his bedroom. I suppose he knew he'd have heard about it if I'd lost or killed the dog. I slept there with my head on Mr Christian's belly, rising and falling, arms around his body, hands weaved into his fur, my feet cool on the slate floor.

Scott kicked me awake on Saturday morning. I could hear the new baby – Peta – crying upstairs.

'Come on, you've got footy today,' he said, his foot lightly tapping up and down my leg. 'And then we've got the state game. Mum said we can go early for the warm-up if we have time.'

'Depends where I'm playing footy,' I groaned, slapping his little leg away.

'Only in Swanbourne, it's not far!'

I looked up at him with squinted eyes. He already had his black-and-gold footy shirt on, with matching shorts and socks.

'Are you playing for us tonight, then?'

He rolled his eyes and kicked at me again. 'Come on, Grant!'

Pippin was in the kitchen making breakfast for Jodee when I was ready to leave. Jodee was no longer the baby, maybe two years old. She never seemed to know who I was.

'Looks like we're catching the train,' I said, bumping Scott with my elbow. He either didn't hear me or didn't care. Hugging his footy tight to his chest, smiling, he followed me out the door.

We weren't even halfway through the second quarter when it happened. This big bloke, who was definitely older than fourteen, tackled me. I was out on the wing on a run and I didn't see him coming. I didn't even have time to brace myself for the fall with my arms, so my face slapped clean down onto the grass. And because we were on the wing, it wasn't soft grass either – it was hard clay underneath. The first thing I remember was tasting metal in the back of my mouth. I rolled over. My whole head ached. I couldn't feel the blood pouring out of my mouth because my face was numb. But running my tongue over the front of my teeth I could feel that something was missing.

It was getting hot by the time Dave picked us up in a paddy wagon and drove us to the emergency dentist. Scott didn't say a word. There was no way we were making it to Subi Oval now. I couldn't even apologise to him with the gauze-wrapped pack of peas keeping the blood inside my mouth. The triage nurses must have taken pity on me because they let us straight through.

'We've had to take the roots out, everything,' the dentist said, addressing me but looking at Dave. 'I can make a plate to fill the gap for now, but your mouth will keep growing.'

It sounded expensive.

'I'm surprised at the severity of the break, honestly,' the dentist added.

I wondered if the structural integrity had been damaged when I first chipped my tooth back at Lyall Street when Pippin slapped the back of my head into the concrete for licking sherbet off the footpath. But I didn't mention it.

While out for a surf at the weekend, I kept my plate on my towel on the beach for safekeeping.

'You look like Alfred E. Neuman,' said Sam. The bloke with the missing tooth from *MAD* magazine.

'Thanks, mate.'

I was trying out my new board. It felt heavier in the water so I had to paddle even harder. Sam had caught at least three waves before I even got close. My arms started to tire but I pushed on until I finally felt it. I pinched my arms by my side and pushed myself up as the wave propelled me forward. The force of the wave was stronger with the heavier board, the board itself more stable. I felt like I was flying.

We stayed out so long I could barely muster the strength to paddle back. Drying myself off with my towel, it took me a moment before I noticed the plate in the sand. In two distinct pieces. The tooth had snapped off it.

'Ah fuck, Mum's going to kill me.'

***

I can't remember when I started work or what I did first, but when I lived at the old police station on Stirling Highway, I worked for the chemist. Mostly I'd ride around on my bike in the afternoons after school, delivering prescription drugs to the old ducks who were too frail to make it to the shop.

Right down to the river, even if it was raining or what. It was good money.

Dave was in the kitchen, looking for the timetable for the train. He didn't usually get called into the city.

'Try the bottom drawer,' said Mum.

The room was uptight.

'Why do they need you there anyway?'

'They put a call out to all of metro. A big protest on the Terrace against the Premier.'

'Why are they protesting?' I asked.

Dave's eyes flashed hot. It didn't matter to him. He left without the timetable.

I scanned the *West* lying open on the dining table, flipping through the pages until I found something that made sense.

COURT'S MINISTER FOUND CORRUPT

'The Premier's refusing to sack the mining minister even though he made money off a government project,' I said to no one.

'Well, I'm not surprised they're angry, then,' said Mum.

***

'Tooth in this time?' asked Sam, paddling just out ahead of me, looking back over his shoulder.

I shrugged, sensing a wave behind me and starting to paddle as hard as I could. I had it this time. The wave propelled me forward and I pushed up from my chest to stand, guiding myself along the wave towards the sand. I paddled back. Sam was fiddling with his leg-rope when a wave crashed right on top of him. His scream was muffled by the water flooding his open mouth. He was spitting and groaning when his head popped back up, his hands draped over his upside-down board. I couldn't help but laugh as he clambered back onto his board. He shot me a look and my head tilted back in uproarious laughter.

And then I felt it drop. My new, new plate. With the tooth attached. Plonked into the ocean.

And then Sam was laughing. Crouched over his board, struggling to breathe. I tried fishing around for it but it was gone.

'Your mum is going to kill you!'

Mum was ropable.

'It was too loose, Mum. It just fell out.'

'Why weren't you more careful with it? You know it cost a bomb!'

'I'm sorry.'

'Well, we probably can't afford another one now. What will Dave say when he gets home? Maybe we should just let them grow together over the gap like the orthodontist said.'

'Mum, I can't have one front tooth!'

I caught Scott's eye across the table. He was trying not to laugh. Now was certainly not the time. Mum silently served up tea. Chops and veg. The chops were tough as anything. I cut into the meat, trying to slice up the smallest amount possible, in order to get it to my – wholly intact – back teeth. I could feel Scott's eyes on me. Mum and Pippin were fussing over Jodee and baby Peta, the former playing hockey with her peas, the latter wriggling around in her highchair. I shoved the tough chop meat on my fork into my mouth and looked up at Scott, staring him dead in the eye, and smiled, the brown meat poking through the vacant tooth hole. Scott spat out his mouthful of peas, laughing. I choked the meat down. Pippin shot us a look. I'm not sure Mum even noticed.

The next day I picked up Sam on the way to the beach. There were some cars parked at the front of the car park with guys standing around them. In jeans, smoking. They looked out of place for Cott. I recognised one of the guys from Hollywood High. He ran around with the skinheads. He was leaning up against a Mini Minor with a huge Union Jack painted on the roof. The closer we got, the louder it was. The skinheads were yelling, jeering at people on the beach. Flicking their cigarettes into the sand. An English accent called out to us as we made our way down.

'This one's got a coon boyfriend!'

I tried to turn around but Sam grabbed me, steering me towards the beach.

We could see some older guys jump them in the car park from where we sat in the ocean, waiting for waves. We even cheered as they flipped their Mini Minor onto its roof, the Union Jack flush against the bitumen. I wondered if Dave was out there with the rest of the cops who came down to break it up. I looked for him but I couldn't tell.

We were in the car, driving home from Ga and Jempa's when Mum said, 'Dave got a job out in Wyalkatchem. We're moving.'

'Where?' Pippin asked.

'Wyalkatchem.'

'Where's that?'

'The country.'

I didn't know what to say.

'I don't want to move to the country,' said Scott.

Mum kept her eyes on the road. She looked tired.

'What the hell am I going to do?' I asked.

'You don't have to come with us, you've got work.'

‘It’s not real work.’

‘Well, there won’t be real work in Wyalkatchem either!’

‘So I can stay?’

‘You can do whatever you want.’

I looked at Scott through the side mirror. He didn’t look back.

That night Dave explained that while I could indeed do whatever I wanted, the old police station on Stirling Highway was on loan to the family from the Cottesloe Police Station. It would be given up to accommodate the incoming chief of police.

‘I suppose I could live with Peter, or Gary,’ I said.

‘And what are you going to do for “real work?”’ Dave asked.

‘Start an apprenticeship or something.’ I didn’t mean it to sound like a question but it came out like one.

I waved goodbye from the front porch. The station wagon was packed with bags and pillows, and cricket gear. The six of them fit perfectly in the car without me. Jodee in the middle bench seat up front with Mum and Dave. The baby squeezed between Scott and Pippin in the back.

I could hear Jodee’s tiny voice from the open window as they pulled out of the driveway.

‘Mummy, is the man not coming with us?’

THE OTHER SIDE OF THE SWAN

I suppose I could start an apprenticeship or something, thought Charlie.

He'd walked down to the river after lunch. It was that time of year where green leaves started to sprout on all the trees again. Charlie's eyes were itchy. He missed the country – the brown rock and red dirt. How clearly you could see the Milky Way in the night sky. He missed being taught by his mum. The kids at school were so loud. Every so often teachers would call on Charlie to answer a question or contribute to a discussion and his face would flush and he'd struggle to get a word out. He could feel the eyes of the other students burning holes into his flesh until red rashes crept up his neck. He didn't mind science. He liked when they got to break into pairs and put on the big coats and safety glasses and work the flame of the Bunsen burner. He'd focus on picking up a little piece of metal with the tongs and holding it over the flame, watching it change colour and shape. And then everything was more still. But mostly he hated school.

He was just off the bike path, in a clearing between the trees and the riverbank that jutted up against a rock wall built like a tiny cliff. A bit further along – to his right – was Point Walter. He knew if he kept going, he'd find people there. He imagined he could hear faint screams of play fights and the splashes of bombies and pin drops from where he stood downriver. He dropped his bag off his back and threw his legs over the edge.

They'd moved back to Perth maybe a year before. It was meant to be home. But Charlie couldn't remember it. All the buildings were new and the same. The limestone blocks that formed the foundation of everything were the same colour as the sand, which was everywhere else. The mildness of it felt strange to him. He missed the humidity and the seasons of the east. The variables. Perth was too clean. Stagnant. Perfect.

From his bag, he pulled out a pouch of tobacco and the little steel tin that used to be surf wax, and started rolling a joint, carefully combining the green and brown in a straight line in the centre of a taut Tally-Ho. It wasn't too windy on the water yet. He lit the end where the paper was rolled up, pinched together. The sun beat down on the river hard, throwing bright white light into the air. There was a wall of light, like fog or a pane of glass, between him and the double- and triple-storeys on the other side of the river. He didn't have a watch so he didn't know what time it was. But he imagined he could hear the school siren, and the clattering of students packing up their notebooks and shoving their pencil cases in their bags. He brushed the tip of his shoe in the river – just in case – to check it was real, and swung his bag over his left shoulder and walked back along the bike path towards the main drag.

The streets were wide in Bicton. Front lawns – a surreal green. No one parked on the verge so the cars lined up on the street. Charlie thought about how many cars were unlocked. How many of the houses were empty. It was too bright. He chanced the handle of an FJ station wagon and the door lurched open. The weight of it shocked him. He slammed it back shut. It was definitely too bright. But he would come back.

The house that was meant to be home had a big wraparound porch that nobody ever sat on. The driveway was painted dark blue. Bottlebrush trees dropped little red florets in piles all over the place. The Hills hoist was in the front yard instead of the back. The yard was shady but not dark.

Charlie could tell his mum was angry by the angle of her spine. She had one hand on the kitchen bench – white-knuckled. The other was upwardly faced, an open envelope between her index finger and thumb. Her back was a cat, arched sideways. She looked like a perverse teapot. Without speaking she passed him the envelope. In it was a letter from school, noting his frequent absences from class. The red-and-white South Fremantle Football Club clock on the wall in the kitchen said two twenty-five, the little hand protruding from the small of the bulldog's back.

She screamed at Charlie until his dad came home, wiping his hands on his overalls and holding his arm outstretched as the letter passed from Charlie's hands to his. His dad read it – quiet – and when he was done, he placed it on the kitchen bench and grabbed a KB of Swan Draught out of the fridge. Charlie's mum was in the lounge room now. He imagined he could hear her, perched on the couch. Knitting. Shaking her head. Muttering under her breath.

Charlie's dad told him how he had never really liked school much himself. It was too noisy. He couldn't concentrate so he'd always be in trouble. His dad told him that he'd work it all out eventually. But until then, he offered to take Charlie along to his next job. He fixed ceilings these days. Layering the panels of insulation and plasterboard. Rendering it over – smooth, white – until it looked like it'd always been there, cutting in cornices at the wall's edge.

The next job was by the beach. In Cottesloe.

It sounded like a change, which was nearly good enough for Charlie.

JOHN STREET

Perth in the seventies was a sleepy old town. Cottesloe especially. It must have been expensive to live there then, like it is now. But it didn't feel like it. It was filled with surfers and young people – incensed by the Vietnam War and broader issues of social justice. A dawning global consciousness was making its way to the most isolated city on earth. When the Whitlam Government was elected in 1972 it felt like the windows had been flung open, and the entire country was breathing in fresh air for the first time. It never rained and it was a dry heat.

Around that time, I was boarding at Gary's place on John Street in Cottesloe. One of those huge, old, character buildings on the hill, where if you stood on your tippy-toes on the wraparound porch, facing west, you could see the faint blue line of the ocean at the end of the street. Gary's mum was a teacher at the primary school. And Gary's old man used to play with Polly Farmer at East Perth.

'Tight as a fish's arse, Polly,' Gary's old man would say. 'Never gave the rest of us a look in.'

When the governor-general declared Australia's participation in the war in Vietnam was over, I started my apprenticeship to become a diesel mechanic. It took me two buses to get to the Technical College on Kensington Street in East Perth. But I didn't mind it there. I found it easier to understand the more tangible and practical examples of maths and physics in college than back at Hollywood High. The tutor, Andrew, was patient with me too – stopping to look over my shoulder at my exercises, at pages streaked with dark blue from the crosses and heavy scratches of my pen over all my mistakes. Andrew was kind. I don't remember much about him other than I could tell he really cared about how we fared and what we were learning.

'Bit ugly but you got there in the end,' he'd say.

***

The sun was rising over the little sliver of blue of the Indian Ocean, visible through the Norfolk pines. Gary and I sat on the porch with our instant coffees. It was just cold enough to have a jumper on. Gary was flicking through the *West Australian* with his left hand, paper spread out over his knees, coffee mug in his right, blowing the steam off the top.

'Swell looks alright,' he said.

Gary's old man had said he'd take us out to Rotto on his boat, so we grabbed our gear and made our way down to the jetty. On the way we saw Sam, dressed in his Christ Church blazer – navy shorts, dress shoes and some sort of musical instrument under his arm – walking towards the train station. Sam was a killer surfer. He was good at every sport, really. Intuition and agility. He's one of the only old boys who still goes out for a paddle even now, I think. With his son in tow.

When he saw us across the road he smiled until he didn't.

'Where are you guys going?' He was staring at our surfboards.

'Rotto.'

We crossed the road to meet him.

'How?'

'The old man,' said Gary.

Without a word Sam turned around and began to lead us down towards the beach, walking quick.

'Give me two minutes,' he said, turning down a side street, pace at a trot. Then he was back. Wetsuit on, surfboard under the arm this time.

'Shall we?'

Gary's old man tied up at Strickland Bay. The water was this intense aquamarine colour. It looked like pure crystal. I didn't realise how comfortable I'd become at Cott until I tried surfing another break. The waves thrashed us around. Sam found his feet first. I think he only nosedived once. When the wind got unbearable, we paddled up to shore and found shelter in the dunes and cracked a few cans. Gary rolled a joint and we smoked it. We paddled back soon after. It must have still been arvo because the sun was high. But Sam had to get home before his old folks did. I didn't mind. I felt more comfortable with my sunglasses on anyway, sitting on the front of the boat, the water spraying my legs dangling over the front. Waves bumping us so hard it felt like the boat could take off into the air.

When I wasn't surfing or at Technical College, I was working on the buses at the Metropolitan Transport Trust – the MTT. Dale, my supervisor, was the kind of old bloke who just didn't want to be there. Whose spirit had left the place years, perhaps decades, before his bodily vessel had the chance to retire. I didn't mind him much, but he wasn't exactly a lot of help. And I felt like I particularly needed that help as an apprentice. But Dale mainly delegated the training to another supervisor Chris, and in turn, his third-year apprentice, Nelson. And they were awful.

It didn't help that Nelson was about six foot five and I was barely out of puberty. Their only redeeming qualities were that they were all in the union. Chris was actually the delegate and in charge of our bargaining. So while he tormented me on the shop floor, he was simultaneously trying to get me a pay rise.

The MTT was this big, open warehouse. Tall enough for two buses stacked on top of one another, at least. There was a carcass of an old train carriage gathering dust in the corner. And a shit-ton of engines and vehicle parts strewn across the warehouse floor. Older men were everywhere, throwing boisterous comments at each other, with booming laughs that echoed in the large space. It had an intimidating energy to it. I fucking hated it.

'Okay, Grant, you crawl up there then. I'll hoist you up,' Chris said one morning, motioning towards the open bonnet of the bus, smoke escaping out of it. He was smirking, his bald head shining under the fluorescent lights of the workshop. I thought he was pretty fucking audacious for a bald guy.

'Is there a harness?' I asked, trying to remember what Andrew had said at college about safety practices in the workshop, and thinking about my gloves and glasses tucked away in my bag in the tearoom.

'She'll be right,' said Chris.

Dale was on the other side of the workshop, flat back on a creeper, head under bus. If he heard what was happening, it didn't appear to stir him. Chris jostled me against the bonnet and grabbed my left leg with both arms while Nelson crouched down and grabbed my right, and together they lifted me up so that my waist was level with the bonnet.

'Lift it up,' one of them yelled.

I lifted the bonnet up and smoke rushed, choking me. I coughed my lungs out. The men lowered me back down, snickering.

'So, is it the engine then?' asked Nelson, smirking. My eyes were watering from the smoke and I couldn't stop coughing.

Chris slapped me on the back. 'Better grab the scissor lift then. To be safe,' he said.

I couldn't say another word that day. And I cried myself to sleep when I eventually got home.

In the water the next day, Sam asked me how it was all going.

'What?' I asked

'The apprenticeship.'

'It's okay, I guess.'

We were out at Cott for a surf, but it was flat so we were just sitting on our boards and kicking our feet. My hand still hurt from where I'd burnt it on the bonnet of the bus.

'There's a guy there giving me shit. Nelson,' I said.

'Nelson who?'

'Nelson Graham.'

'Two first names.'

'Exactly.'

A school of tiny fish swam underneath us. Seaweed felt like jellyfish wrapped around our legs.

'Do you think you could do it forever?' Sam asked.

'I don't know.'

A wave was in danger of forming but it reconsidered.

When we got back to the Cott Hotel, Pope was holding court.

'Where's the dog?' he asked as Sam and I pulled up to his table.

'In the country with the family.'

'That's a shame. He's a good boy.'

Some of the old blokes nodded and grunted.

'Have you told Sam about the time you got done playing two-up?' I said.

A few of the blokes nodded and groaned in agreement. We all loved that story. Pope set his pint down and looked at Sam, delighted in his new audience.

'Well firstly, we'd been playing two-up since the Second World War, so I wasn't aware that it was even a crime,' Pope started, eyes bright. 'So when the coppers stormed in here on Anzac Day a couple of years back with bloody rifles pointed at me and the other diggers, I nearly well fell off my chair. It was the shock of it that made me put up such a fight, I think.'

'What happened?' asked Sam.

'They bloody well arrested us. Took us down to the East Perth lock-up and all! And confiscated the float, for God's sake.'

'Un-Australian!' shouted an old bloke, the others grunting in agreement.

'Yeah well, they regretted that after all, didn't they, the coppers. Had me on Channel Seven news that night and the premier called my telephone the next day.'

The old blokes roared again, charging their pints.

'And it's legal now, two-up,' I said to Sam.

'Only on Anzac Day,' said Pope.

***

I was stuck working late at the MTT again. Dale had a fishing trip or a cricket match or something on that weekend, so he left early. I was lying on my back on the creeper, my head under the bus. I was used to Nelson mucking around with me while I was working under there so I didn't even notice that he had taken my shoes off until he had wheeled me out, pinning me down while Chris stripped down my overalls. I struggled but Nelson had me tight by the arms. I was too scared to scream. Chris's arm darted under the bus and back, his hand holding a lump of solid grease.

'Flip him over,' Chris said.

Nelson wrestled me to the ground, my face flat against the concrete, one arm still on the creeper, overalls around my ankles.

'Alright, grease him,' said Nelson. And Chris slapped his hand full of grease against my balls, rubbing the grease all over them. I started to scream then. They laughed. I waited for a long time before getting up just to make sure they'd gone. The bus trip home seemed to last days. My eyes stung from crying.

That night Peter and I went to a party at a share house on Marine Parade. It was more of a mansion than a house really. It was a grand old limestone design with separate apartments underneath and a huge verandah out the back, enclosed. Right on the beach. A band was setting up in the front room when we got there. The front room was huge, with chocolate brown and green paisley carpet, records littered everywhere and guitars leaning up against amps and walls. Peter rolled a joint and we smoked it out on the front lawn. The sounds of the band's opening chords came from the front room and carried over the water so that it sounded like it was coming from the beach.

Towards the middle of third term, Technical College started to bore me. I soon got the hang of the equations, so Andrew spent less time trying to help me. And whenever I spent time in class all it did was remind me how much I hated going back to work at the MTT. The exam was scheduled for a Friday. I don't remember much about studying much for the exam except the hours spent the night before collating and perfecting a cheat sheet of equations to guide me through. I felt calm in the exam room, flipping through the pages when the time began and methodically making my way through the questions. I passed. Even though Andrew had marked the exams simply 'pass' or 'fail' with no feedback or criticisms, I knew I'd done well. When we received our marks, Peter's mum and old man put on a lamb roast to celebrate.

'Well done, Grant. You'll be a diesel mechanic in no time,' said Gary's old man, stubby of Swan held up in a salute.

'Well done, mate,' said Gary, clinking his stubby against mine. The food and beer were so good and Gary's family so kind, but I couldn't relax my shoulders or relieve the pit of anxiety in my chest. I had to go back to work at the MTT tomorrow. I even went to bed before sweets.

I decided to call in sick to work at the MTT the next day. Dale was pissed off with me.

'Mate, it's not a very good look to be chucking a sicky as an apprentice,' he said. 'There's plenty of other young blokes desperate for work around here who'd love your position and who'd never have the cheek.'

'I'm sorry,' I said.

‘Don’t make a habit of it.’

I went back to bed until I heard Gary’s old man leave. Then I went to the beach.

I remember feeling guilty all the time. The guilt just sat there, in the pit of my stomach. It’s easy to look back now and see I was being bullied, and that there were other avenues out there I could try. But at the time, it felt like my world was ending. And there was no way out.

That weekend Peter and I went to Darcy’s eighteenth birthday in Freo. Darcy played footy with Scott, and I’d seen his brother out surfing at Cott too. They were real characters. I remember I was excited for it. There were a few people I knew from Hollywood High, most of the guys from Cott there, and some people I didn’t recognise at all. Everyone was smoking pot.

There was a mass of people sitting around in the front room passing pipes and bongs around. I sat in there for hours. Robert, Darcy’s brother, was packing the cones, always engrossed in hysterical conversation. His laugh was intoxicating. I don’t remember how we got home that night but I ended up picking up an ounce from Robert. It stank out my jacket. When I got home, I stole one of Gary’s mum’s airtight Tupperware containers to store it in. I still imagined I could smell it though.

As soon as I walked into the workshop at the MTT, Nelson started giving me shit.

'Here's our sickly child. Had a turn, did you?' he sneered.

'Fuck off,' I said.

'Language, mate!' barked Dale.

Nelson and Chris shared a smile at my expense. One of the southern route buses had blown up on Stock Road so it was all hands on deck. It was one of those days where you're so busy that you forget that you hate your job. If Nelson was trying to rile me up, I didn't notice. Until we started packing up the workshop and Nelson stood over me, greasy hands pressing on my shoulders, and whispered in my ear.

'You're dead, cunt.'

I walked at a clip to my car at shift's end, grateful I no longer had to wait for the bus.

Down at Cott some of the older guys were out on the water. James was there. And his mate Ralphy. They caught waves like it was automatic. We stayed out longer than we usually did, just to watch. When I got home, I realised I had an assignment for Technical College due that day. I hadn't even started it. I skipped class the next day to write it and by the time I handed it in, Andrew knocked twenty per cent off the mark. I still passed. Andrew didn't say anything about it, but I felt ashamed anyway.

I sat by the Swan River, sort of where the baths used to be, and stared into the murky brown water. It must have been my dad, years earlier, who'd warned me about the sharks in there. I imagined them under the salty brown water. I imagined myself submerged in it. Eyes burning from the salt. Swimming the wrong direction, away from the light.

It was Debbie's eighteenth birthday party that night, in Mossie Park. Debbie's parents must have been loaded. It was one of those houses right on the river, with a big open balcony and a TV outside. Debbie was cool though. You wouldn't know she was rich. Sam was there, leaning against the back of the couch, brushing his shaggy hair out of his eyes. He must have snuck out of the house. Or maybe his folks were out. I brought half of the ounce with me and sold it off to people at the party. I sank a few beers. I was starting to get tired and had footy the next day, so I left before midnight. I can't remember whose car it was, Peter's maybe, or who else was in the car. All I remember is I was driving home to John Street and somewhere along Stirling Highway a copper pulled me over and pinged me for drink driving. I felt a release when he put me in the back seat of the car like my body was relaxing. I was no longer in control. I just sat there, feeling the cool leather of the car seat against my arms and watched little droplets of rain roll across the window.

At the East Perth lock-up they asked me for a number to

call to come pick me up. It was too late to call Gary's house. It was pointless calling Mum. And I vaguely hoped that Dave wouldn't find out because it wasn't in his bailiwick. So I gave the only other number I could remember off the top of my head and Pope came within the hour to bail me out.

'Well you won't be doing this again in a hurry, will you,' Pope said, more than asked.

The roads were quiet now. It was still raining.

'Your old man won't be happy. They might drag you out to the country to keep an eye on you.'

I didn't even allow myself to wonder if I'd be better off in the country. I wanted to tell Pope that they didn't want me there. Or want me at all. But I didn't say anything, just sat there.

Mum rang the next morning at eight am.

'What were you thinking, Grant?'

I mumbled something in response, I don't really remember what. I mostly just let her yell at me.

'Someone in Perth faxed your mugshot straight to the station in Wylie last night! Dave was mortified.'

It didn't feel it necessary to fill the silence when she stopped screaming to clamber for air.

'I've never known anyone so selfish.'

She hung up on me at some point. I would have liked to speak to Scott or Pippin but I didn't bother ringing back.

When the sun set, I got drunk at the beach. It was as cold as it gets for Perth so it was quiet. The sand was cool against my skin. The water was so blue it was black. The Jack Daniel's warmed my chest, and the joint I smoked tingled and buzzed my skin and relaxed my bones. I lay on the sand staring up at the sky. I tried to map patterns in the stars but I only really knew the Southern Cross. I imagined myself there one thousand years earlier looking at the same sky and stars, and my heart ached.

I didn't go back to the MTT after that. I didn't quit. I didn't even let Dale know. I just never went back.

PART TWO

1975–1982

BY THE KOSHI RIVER

It was so humid outside that Charlie lay across the bed with a wet towel draped over his naked torso and the ceiling fan on full pelt. Susie had gone down to the markets. He'd offered to go with her but his heart really wasn't in it – he'd spent enough time being hassled by salesmen when they were in South-East Asia before. He'd been swindled into buying every wooden carving, ivory figure and Buddhist idol there was. He supposed he probably could use a fresh packet of cigarettes at least. So he had offered to accompany her, the smallest act of chivalry for the greatest of sacrifices she was about to make for him. But Susie insisted on going alone.

At three pm the clock radio on the bedside table – the black, rectangular box with the red digits that every hotel or motel room on earth seemed to have – sounded its alarm.

Charlie rocked himself up, sliding his feet into his thongs and picking up whatever shirt was top of the pile in his suitcase. The humidity slapped at him as soon as he opened the front door. He lit a cigarette to take his mind off of it.

The restaurant was just up the road. It was one of those small, homely Himalayan restaurants. You could tell it was good because it was full of locals, and none of the menus were in English. Charlie picked the table closest to the window and waited. He quietly, subtly glanced at each face around the room. No one was carrying anything on them. None met his eye. In fact the only eye he seemed to catch was King Birendra's, whose colourful portrait hung just above the kitchen door.

After at least an hour, the kitchen door swung open and a man in chef's clothes, carrying a paper bag of what looked like takeaway food, sat opposite Charlie, by the window. He didn't say much, the man. He just placed the paper-bagged package in the middle of the table, pointed his finger at it and said, 'Half.' Charlie nodded, like it was all fairly self-explanatory.

'And the rest?' he asked.

'Saturday,' said the man. He gave Charlie a piece of paper, on which was written the details of a place in the highlands.

A young girl came over then, with a pot of tea in hand. She quietly filled the tiny, white, round teacups in front of the men. One hand rested behind the small of her back as she poured. The hand that clutched the teapot was shaking. The men drank their tea in silence. Then the man left. As did Charlie, brown paper package tucked tightly under his sweaty arm.

When Charlie got back to the villa, Susie was in the kitchen, sarong tied loosely around her waist, wearing nothing on top. He dropped the package on the dining-room table next to a tower of fresh cigarettes and wrapped his arms around her, resting his chin on her shoulder.

He could get used to this, Charlie thought.

They dipped into the stash to check the quality and sank into each other and themselves and fucked all night.

In the morning they went on a hike through the valley. It was hot. And humid. Charlie used the time to wargame their journey home. First playing out the scenario in his head, step by step, and then relaying the information to Susie, piece by piece. How they'd hide the product in their bodies. How they'd act in the airport. How many times they'd need to go to the bathroom on the flight. Where they'd take the taxi to first when back in Perth, rather than to their homes. What would happen if they got caught. Charlie was cautious in his speech, half expecting Susie to run away from him at first chance. But Susie was fearless. She didn't say much, just nodded along, breaking into smiles to punctuate the silences.

The trail was mostly cleared from the earthquake, but there were piles of debris stacked on the forest edge which threatened to spill out at every corner. The earth was hard, then soft in many places. The pine trees were so tall you couldn't see the peaks of them. Little trails veered off the main one to hidden Buddhist temples each topped with seven with ancient pagoda roofs, sporting ornate wooden architectural structures. Charlie watched as Susie ran her hands over the wooden carvings, feeling the ridges under her fingertips, imagining the workers poring over their artwork for a lifetime.

When they reached the end of the trail they found the Koshi River. It was flanked by a small market. Here, among the little stalls selling ivory and wooden figures and little trinkets were animals on display. A rhinoceros in a locked wooden box. A red panda, chained up. An elephant with a heavy iron bracelet around its leg. Tourists lined up to touch the animals. The handlers had sharp instruments that they'd plough into the animals' ribs if they threatened to move or nip. Charlie looked at Susie. She was clearly devastated. He led her away quickly by the hand.

They went the long way back. Through another trail flanked by barley and maize fields. Workers toiling away, slicing down the tall crops with machetes.

When they got home they got high and fucked again. Then Susie cried.

They sat out the front of the villa on plastic chairs overlooking the forest until the sun started to creep up on Saturday morning. Charlie kicked on his motorbike. He didn't have on any protective gear or leathers. Not even a helmet. Just a fag hanging out the side of his mouth, and double pluggers. Susie leaned over him and kissed his cheek as the engine roared.

Charlie smiled up at Susie. She was crying again. She looked bloody beautiful.

MARINE PARADE

On 11 November 1975 the governor-general sacked the Whitlam Government. The whole country was in shock. This was before the twenty-four-hour news cycle and the social media hysteria that plagues contemporary politics. People rarely heard from the government until it was election time. I couldn't believe that the representative of the Queen, of all people, had dismissed our prime minister – who we'd voted for. I felt powerless. And angry.

Around that time I wound up moving into that share house on Marine Parade – the one from the party with Peter. Six of us were living there – Laurie, Brett, Johnny, Michael, Darcy and me. Laurie was a huge, funny Liberian guy and a great cook. Brett, who I knew from Hollywood High, was into surfing and partying too. I knew Johnny and Michael from parties at the share house I had been to in the past. Then there was Darcy and me. But there were always more than six people in the house. Peter, for example, never paid any rent but he may as well have lived there too. Musos and surfers abounded. Coming home, you knew there'd be a crew sitting out on the verandah having a sesh. We were so close to the beach that you could see what the swell was like from the kitchen. And there were always guitars lying around, so I started teaching myself how to play.

Laurie loved his food. He worked out we could go down to Bruno's greengrocers on a Saturday when they were shut down and knock off free vegetables. So Sunday through Tuesday we'd eat like kings on Laurie's cooking. He'd make beautiful curries and stir fries and stews. But food never lasted long in that house. Beer and cigarettes usually got us to the end of the week.

I was on the dole, but I had a few cash-in-hand jobs here and there. For a while I worked making nylon rope. It was me and a bunch of Vietnamese women, in a workshop in North Fremantle. Pulling and pouring tiny beads of plastic – polycaproamide – in one end and then extruding it out, through water, into hot, stretched, melted string. We'd coil it up like fishing line, and then the machine would take the coils and wind them into rope. It was hot and gave me calluses on my fingers. We didn't even wear gloves. But the Vietnamese women were always bringing me in food, so I never had to buy lunch. Then one day the place just shut down. I went in and it was all boarded up, no sign or anything.

After that I got a job tiling floors. I sort of landed in that job really. Snail, one of Darcy's brother's mates, was talking about doing slate floors around Mosman Park with him and a few of the old boys from the deaf school. The first house I worked on was a Kailis family house. Old Kailis was there and helped us mix the grout. It was hard work, bending over like that. Good money, though. And I was pretty good at it, I think. At least they kept me on when they gave Snail the sack. He was a bit slow, old Snail.

The blow-up pool out the back of Marine Parade was growing tadpoles. The lounge room always looked like a battlefield, strewn with bodies on the couches and on the floor. I had to identify a path through the sleeping bodies, tiptoeing my way through like it was a minefield. Emu Export cans were everywhere. I tried picking one up to clean up a bit, but it was too overwhelming so I put it straight back down on the bench and didn't even bother looking for the bin. The fridge was empty, save for an old pizza box. On the verandah I picked up a half-empty packet of smokes and took one. Darcy was out there, packing a cone and smiling to himself.

'What was the occasion?' I asked.

'No occasion,' he said.

His bong was a Harvey Fresh orange juice bottle with the label half ripped off and a short piece of dark-green garden hose protruding out of it. The water in it was dark brown.

'Probably about due for an upgrade.'

I put my cigarette out in the ashtray. Darcy lit the little makeshift cone piece, made of aluminium foil, on the end of the hose and inhaled deeply, resulting in loud gurgling, sucking and bubbling sounds followed by an eruption of smoke out of his mouth and nose.

'Probably,' said Darcy.

Marine Parade was such an old build and so lacking in insulation that it was a thermometer. It could be six am in the lounge room and one of the boys would lick his index finger and hold it up, and announce the weather outside. Even though time is relative, and especially so there, we kind of kept up with the seasons by how livable the house was at any one particular time.

Sam was always hanging around, in his Christ Church school uniform. I think he'd given up the trumpet by then, or whatever the hell it was he'd been playing. Sam just had this natural ability to speak and relate with anyone. Maybe that's empathy. I don't know. I loved having him around, though. It felt like home.

When it got too cold to surf – for me anyway – I built an electric guitar out of old bits. Michael helped me. He was good at electronics and had all these discarded pieces lying around. I soldered it together. But he knew how to keep the neck straight and change out the pickups and everything. We jammed with it. It had a pretty cool sound. I had a little nylon acoustic guitar too. The guy who lived next door was learning to play, so we jammed with him. And Michael and Johnny. And anyone else who would swing by, like Dom Mariani out of The Stems. Most of us were learning, so it was very laissez faire. And we smoked a lot of pot.

I don't remember exactly when, but it was on Marine Parade that I first saw someone doing heroin. One of Johnny's friends had brought it over. A few of the musos were into it, I suppose. Looking back, I feel like I should have been shocked by the sight of someone tying their arm up with a belt and injecting themselves with a shock of brown liquid in my front room. But it didn't seem out of place there at Marine Parade.

I was glad the gear was gone, though, when Sam came around the next day to coax me out for a surf.

'How's the family?' he asked.

We were at the southern end of the break because, being a Saturday, the main break was too crowded. Even though it was fucking freezing. Sam could only surf weekends these days, busy with school. I hadn't realised that I hadn't spoken with my family for months until he posed that question.

'I don't know,' I said.

I used the phone at the Cott Hotel to call the Wylie police station. I got through to Scott.

'How's it going?'

'Yeah good,' he said. 'We're top of the ladder at footy. Nearly done with school.'

'That's great.'

'Are you still playing?'

'Footy? Yeah, rezzies for Swanbourne.'

'How's it going?'

'Should make finals.'

'We might be back for the cricket season. Dave's looking at other posts.'

'I'll see you at Christmas anyway.'

I could hear someone calling him from the other end. His hand over the receiver couldn't mask the question.

'Mum, do you want to talk to Grant?'

Laurie and Darcy had word of a big party. Michael and I had been jamming. I wasn't exactly dressed for a big night, but I decided to go anyway. At this point I'd lost my third plate, so had a missing front tooth until I got my bridge set in the following year. The boardies and thongs were the least of my problems. We parked up out front of a mansion on

Victoria Avenue, Dalkeith. Alan Bond's house. Bond has since become a symbol for a booming Perth in the 1980s, and a cautionary tale against greed and extravagance. Bond went from winning the America's Cup to media mogul to a slew of legal battles and, eventually, imprisonment. But at the time he was on the up.

It was the twenty-first of Bond's son John. The party was in the basement, beneath the underground car park. We could hear Loaded Dice playing when we stepped out of the car, and it got louder still as we made our way into the car park. Darcy led us to the staircase that led to the basement, through the collection of luxury cars. Aston Martins. Porsches. I hadn't felt self-conscious about my missing tooth until that moment. Michael elbowed me in the ribs and pointed to a bright-red Ferrari. Its keys were in the ignition. We stopped for about a second before we kept up walking, laughing at the absurdity of it all.

In July 1976 the Australian Council of Trade Unions organised a nationwide strike over the government's attacks on Whitlam's universal health care system, Medibank. I don't think I even had a job on that day, but I remember sitting with a beer on the verandah and listening to the radio and feeling a strange moment of oneness with all the workers in the country. The ACTU got the trains and buses shut down, factories and everything. Teachers didn't rock up to school. Apparently two million workers walked off the job. It cost the economy half a billion dollars. It's hard to describe the feeling really. I know it's called solidarity, but it felt like something else to me. Something close to belonging.

***

There was a blowfly just hanging around at Marine Parade. I say one, but there must have been a few. It just felt like the same guy bugging me. It would be quiet, then a humming, buzzing sound would come into focus. Then you'd see him, the big, fat, black blowfly. You'd backhand him away, and for a few moments there'd be peace. Then the fucker would start back up again. It must have been spring.

Around then, Peter announced to whoever was hanging around, 'Ralphy's back from Europe and he's got a huge stash.'

'A huge stash of what?' I asked.

We were stretched out on the verandah having medicinal beers, licking our wounds from the night before.

'Heroin,' said Peter.

'From where?'

'Europe. Spain or something. He's been going to bring some around.'

In the arvo, Ralphy came around to Marine Parade with his heroin stash. Just a few little bags of crushed-up near-white powder. He cut it up with a credit card on the coffee table and mixed it around with water in a bottle top until it turned brown. He collected the liquid with a syringe, flicking the barrel a couple of times before holding it up to inspect it. He had one of those bright-patterned fabric belts I'd only ever seen nurses use for a blood test. I can't remember if I went first now, but I distinctly remember it was Ralphy who tied the fabric belt around my bicep and pulled it tight. He flicked the underside of my elbow and passed me the needle, steering my hand in order to guide it in. I felt the pinch of the needle. When Ralphy undid the belt, I felt like I'd fallen into a hot bath. At the same time, I remember feeling nothing, not even my own skin. I felt so light I thought I was dead.

I suppose this should have felt like a turning point. If not then, perhaps upon reflection. But it doesn't, even now. Because I feel like everything in my life has been a slow burn. It started before I was born. I entered it too late.

When the nights had just started to be sticky and unbearable in the house without a fan on, Brett and I had a big party for our twentieth birthdays. We set up a stage in the front room at Marine Parade where The Elks were playing. There were about a hundred people there, spilling out all over the place and onto the road. It was that time of year where it just starts to get warm again, and all the jacarandas are blooming and the air smells like bottlebrushes. Royal Show weather. Pippin was back in town after moving out of Mum and Dave's in Wylie, so she was there, but I didn't remember inviting her. Everyone was there I suppose.

Ralphy was on the verandah out the back, having a smoke. I clinked my can of Export against his in solidarity.

'Grant, how are we?'

'Good, mate.'

'What are you doing for work these days?'

'Nothing really. Odd jobs tiling, but it's dried up.'

He raised an eyebrow. 'I've still got that stash. Why don't you unload it for me?'

I waited for him to continue.

'I don't have time to do it myself anyway. You can make a bit off the bags and that should keep you going.'

I tried to think of a reason to say no but I couldn't.

Bag of Bones started up playing in the front room. So many people were crowded around the makeshift stage that I could barely see the band. I could see Sam in the lounge room mosh pit, though. And Peter. I stayed for the set and went outside for another cigarette.

'Hey mate, do you have a light?'

I turned around to a man far too well dressed to be at Marine Parade by choice. He had a crisp white shirt on with sleeves rolled up to his elbows, slacks and brown shoes. He looked like Frank Sinatra. Or a cop.

'Are you a cop?' I asked, passing him my lighter.

He laughed. 'I'm Charlie.' He smiled with his eyes.

'Grant.'

We shook hands.

'Bag of Bones are great, aren't they? I saw them at the Albion in May, I think it was.'

'I was there too.'

'Great gig. Do you play?'

'I'm learning. Do you?'

'I listen.' He was warm. 'This is my wife, Susie,' he said, placing his arm around her shoulders. She had bleached blonde hair and dark eyes and an electric smile.

'Nice to meet you,' she said. She was warm too.

'We'll see you around,' said Charlie.

I didn't doubt it.

I was down at the beach when the cops finally shut down the party. I was glad I wasn't there to see it. I was sure Pippin had left well before then. I hoped so, anyway. Otherwise we were both fucked if Dave found out. Almost everyone was gone by the time I got back. Brett and Laurie were on the verandah, smoking, still sinking beers.

'What time's the game tomorrow?' I asked.

'Well technically it's today,' said Brett. 'And it's at one pm.'

'Godspeed.'

We played at Claremont Oval, after the league guys had had a run. The sun was right above us when we ran out for the warm-up, and it was bloody hot. We must have been playing Claremont, but it could have been Floreat – I don't remember now. But I distinctly remember praying for the sun to move beyond the grandstand and looking out at the faint peak of the Claremont Hotel just beyond the train station. Its siren call begging me inside for a pint.

The game was a slog. Coach moved me to the backline at half-time just to have an extra man down there, but it didn't make a difference. I had a spew at three-quarter time. Then we lost. The boys were shattered.

We backed it up on Mad Monday. The team started drinking at nine am at the footy club. Around eleven am we hit the Mosman Park Bowling Club. I'm no good at bowls. I had a bit of luck in pool at the Claremont later on, though. God knows what time it was when we got to the Albion, maybe five pm. Laurie had joined us by then. The Albion was a colonial-style building, a real old Australian hotel. It looked like it was dropped there in the gold rush. But it was our haunt.

It was quiet enough but there was still a bouncer on the door. He let most of us through but stopped Laurie.

'You're not coming in here,' he said. He sounded like Tony Greig, with his clipped South African accent.

'Because he's black?' asked Peter from behind the bouncer's back.

The bouncer shrugged. Peter pounced on him then, arm around his neck in a headlock, and wrestled him to the floor. Laurie had legged it halfway down Stirling Highway before we caught up with him. Brett had a spew right there on the footpath. I wasn't far off.

'Fucking South Africans,' said Peter shaking his head. 'Someone needs to tell them we don't have apartheid here.'

'We're probably not far off,' said Laurie.

***

I started playing guitar for The Suspects. Not lead or anything, and just part-time. Michael and Robert played with us too, with Peter on drums. Robert and I weren't the best at keeping up with practice. I had also picked up a bit of work tiling again. But every time we missed a practice session, they cracked the shits. In the end, Michael was the only one of us who didn't get the sack, but it was fun gigging and learning from those guys while it lasted.

It was now so hot in the house that it was more comfortable to sleep on the verandah. Except it was nearly always occupied. At the very least, at all times, by shirtless men and bong smoke.

One time I saw Darcy out there, legs up on an esky, wearing nothing but stubbies and Ray-Bans.

'You guys have been out here for days now,' I said. 'Don't you have a dole cheque to pick up?'

Darcy didn't even flinch. A couple of the other boys laughed.

'We've kept a loose handle on the time by counting how many episodes of *Skippy* we've watched,' said Michael, motioning at the TV.

'How many?' I asked.

'Eight thus far,' said Darcy.

I went inside and into the kitchen. Dirty dishes were piled up in the sink, spilling out over the bench. The pot Laurie used for his chilli last Wednesday was still soaking. I couldn't find a glass or a mug or even a jug to fetch a glass of water. But I refused to wash one up. I was drinking out of the kettle when Michael walked into the kitchen, took one look at the sink and turned back around.

'I have a dream ... that one day we'll have our dishes without needing to clean them first,' he said.

I tiptoed through the mass of sleeping people in the lounge room. The verandah was empty, so I picked up a packet of half-finished cigarettes and had a smoke alone. I grabbed my board and wandered down to the beach. The sun was only just rising. There were no waves so I just sat on my board, looking back up at Marine Parade. The house looked so still.

AN ARTIST'S STUDIO IN NORTH FREO

I had some unpaid fines – parking fines, speeding fines, registration fines, licence fines (or lack thereof). Everything really. And the debt was just accumulating. A couple of the boys told me you could do time to pay it off. Every day you're in, they pay off your debt, they said. So I did about a month at Fremantle Prison.

When I first got out, I crashed at Darcy's mum's place. Lois was an artist. She was warm and kind and felt like a mother. She lived in her studio in North Fremantle, just down the road from The Stoned Crow. From the front verandah looking west you could see down to the Norfolk pines which framed Leighton Beach, flanked by Fremantle Port to its south, and the train station to the north. I remember

Lois pointing to the port and telling me about the MUA, the wharfies' union that banned shipments to South Africa after a massacre of black students there.

Straight ahead was a big industrial area, where I'd worked on the nylon rope a few years earlier. Big warehouses and workshops, and the big Dingo Flour mill. Every white surface stained red with bore water. Out on the horizon was the faint outline of Rotto. Lois let me crash upstairs at her shop. She was so nice. She made these conceptual, almost cubist, portraits out of chalk and oil pastels. Lifelike figures without faces. Line drawings with colour and texture bursting out of them. The colours were sublime but the faceless figures made me feel lonely.

It must have been early 1978. The Dismissal of the Whitlam Government was there in the zeitgeist – we talked about it, but everyone was used to Fraser already. No one was viscerally angry anymore. It was the last decade of the Cold War, and the threat of nuclear destruction was in the back of everyone's minds the world over. Lois was going to protests against uranium mining and that kind of thing. But I was on my own route to self-destruction so I didn't give a fuck.

I started unloading Ralphy's heroin for him. He kept it in the door of a parked car down the side of his house in Mosman Park. Peter and I would head over before and jimmy our arms through the window, pulling out however many packets we thought we'd need. It was easier when Peter was with me because his arms were longer. We'd pick it up before the weekend usually. Or midweek if there was a gig on. Ralphy let me skim a little money and a little dope off the top. It wasn't much, but it helped me pay board to Lois. It was the first time I'd seen a fifty-dollar note, actually. Bright yellow paper. Pineapples, Charlie called them.

I suppose it was around then that I started shooting up fairly regularly. I'd bring it along to gigs at the Albion or Steves or whatever. People were always calling me, asking me to bring it down. But then whatever I didn't sell on the weekend seemed to go too. When Robert and Michael and I were playing music, we'd dip into the stash. Then I started doing it alone. I liked the feeling of letting go of myself, feeling the warmth pull over me like a doona and just sitting with it – not having to speak to anyone, or even look at anyone else. I could just be with myself. It felt like when you catch a wave – that moment you are propelled forward and the wave just takes you and nothing else exists.

I bought a motorbike with the money I'd saved running Ralphy's heroin. A Triumph Thunderbird. It made it far easier to get around to gigs and push the gear. There was an odd symmetry riding through the western suburbs with little packets of heroin in my pockets, where I'd done the same job for the local pharmacy all those years earlier. I didn't feel all that different, really. I couldn't afford to get motorbike lessons or take the test so I didn't have my licence.

'Aren't you scared of getting pulled over?' Sam asked me once.

I suppose I felt like I had nothing to lose.

***

Mum called me on Easter Sunday.

'We're moving back,' she said.

'To Perth?'

'To Rottnest.'

'What?' I wasn't sure I'd heard her correctly.

'Dave's chief of police on Rottnest Island. The girls will be going to primary school there.'

It felt strange to me to imagine Jodee and Peta at school. In my mind they were babies still.

'I didn't know anyone lived there.'

I hadn't been to Rotto since that time on Peter's old man's boat.

'Well, they do. We'll have you over shortly. I'll call you from the island,' she said before hanging up, forgetting to put Scott or Pippin on the phone.

I missed my brothers and sisters. I couldn't help but

imagine all the growing up they were doing without me. I must have been depressed, but the dope numbed it all. Like there was a shower curtain drawn between me and my soul.

On Anzac Day long weekend, The Suspects had a gig at Steves Bar. We did a little warm-up run-through before the gig and sounded like shit.

'Grant, haven't you been practising, mate?' someone said.

Considering all the time I'd had in the loft at Lois's place fucking around, I thought I'd practised quite a bit. But I was starting to lose my sense of time. To be fair, Michael sounded equally as shit. Pete's drumming, however, was flawless.

'Sorry guys, can we run through again?'

I found my rhythm in time for our set. Then they sacked me straight after. They didn't sack Michael, though, which pissed me off at the time.

I went out for a smoke in the beer garden. Charlie was there, smiling. He passed me his lighter.

'I was wondering when I'd see you again,' he said.

'I've been around,' I said.

'How long have you been playing with them?' he said, motioning inside the bar.

'Not very long. Or frequently. Can you tell?

Charlie laughed.

'Anyway, I'm getting out of here.'

'Come over to ours. Susie is making tea,' he said.

Charlie drove to his and Susie's house in Cottesloe, and I followed behind him on my Thunderbird. When we parked up at the driveway, he walked over to me and rested his hand on the handlebars, smiling.

'I used to have one like this.'

'I didn't know you rode.'

He led me through the garage and flicked on the light. There was a pristine Triumph Bonneville Silver Jubilee.

'I don't get out as much as I used to.'

Susie was in the lounge room, dancing, whisky in hand. The Doors were playing 'LA Woman'. A rich smell was emanating from the kitchen – garlic and oregano maybe. I couldn't remember the last time I ate a home-cooked meal. Probably not since Laurie the Liberian's stews. She smiled at Charlie and kissed me on the cheek.

'In Asia you pretty well have to get around on a bike.'

Charlie grabbed a bottle of red and started twisting and driving the silver spiral down into the cork. 'We spent some time in Nepal and I got around on a shitty little Honda. Picked it up from there.' He uncorked the bottle and poured us each a glass. I assumed the wine was expensive by virtue of it not coming out of a cask.

'It's French,' he said.

The walls were covered with black-and-white photographs.

Mostly of Charlie and Susie, with exotic backdrops of waterfalls and mountains, or flanked by temples or elephants. The music stopped then. You could just hear the scratching of the needle against the plastic. Charlie nodded his head towards the record stand. Hundreds of records, stacked neatly in place.

'Your pick,' he said.

I picked up The Rolling Stones' *Exile on Main St.*

'I love this album. I saw them play it at Randwick.'

I didn't know what to say so I just laughed. 'I've never been on a plane,' I said.

I didn't even notice Susie had left the room until she was back with dinner in her arms.

'We are lucky men, thank you, darling,' Charlie said as Susie handed us cutlery and bowls of pasta.

'Thank you, Susie.'

'You are lucky. Usually it's him cooking,' she said, winking at Charlie.

We were onto our second bottle of nice red when Charlie changed the record.

'What is this?'

'It's Tchaikovsky.'

'It sounds triumphant.'

'It is.'

We finished another bottle. Every time I blinked it was

harder to open my eyes back up. When Charlie or Susie moved around or left the room I held them shut, opening them again only when addressed.

'I'm heading to Sydney tomorrow,' Charlie said. 'For a while. I'll get in touch when I'm back.'

The words sounded foreign to me. I just nodded.

'Stay here the night.'

I leaned back into the mound of pillows on the couch and was already half asleep when Susie draped a blanket over me.

'Goodnight, darling,' she said. I thought I felt a kiss on my forehead but I wasn't sure.

***

I was now getting calls left, right and centre about Ralphy's heroin. Word must have gotten around. It was kind of nice, because whenever people would call me up looking for it, they'd invite me along to whatever gig or party was on which they needed the dope for. So it was a boon for my social life in that respect. However, there was very little left at the end of the weekends for personal use. So that was a drag.

The little loft at Lois's felt like home. It was small quarters – just a bed, some clothes racks and a pointed roof with exposed wooden beams that I'd smack my head against if I sat bolt upright. But it had an old, comforting vibe.

It reminded me of Ga's place. I guess I must be genetically predisposed to tight lodgings.

It was my twenty-first birthday in September that year. Mum organised a party for me at Rotto – at the police station. I felt sick the whole ferry ride over. I hadn't spoken to her since March, and I hadn't spoken to anyone else that year. I also had gear on me and was dying to hit it, but I was not about to chance it on water. As soon as we got off the ferry I lit up a cigarette. It was just me and Peter. Mum said to invite along whoever I liked but I kind of forgot about it.

We clambered onto the jetty with the other passengers at about three pm. Imported-looking Norfolk pines jutted out along the shoreline, swaying against the wind. We walked into the bowels of the island, dodging cyclists and children. Everything was sand and sandy limestone. Quokkas were scavenging in front of cafes. The chalets a burnt-orange in the sun. The old chapel stood starkly white against the blue sky. Nothing on the island had changed at all.

When we got to the police station I realised quickly there was nowhere to shoot up there either. The inside toilet was for the women. And the outside toilet for the men was not a toilet but rather a drain cavity by the outdoor laundry with a shower curtain for modesty. Dave's mother, Maureen, was sitting on a plastic chair, chain-smoking cigarettes right by the laundry too, intermittently reaching her hand under the curtain to flick her cigarette ash down the drain. So it was hardly private.

Scott handed me a beer. He looked older. He'd grown his hair longer, into a mullet.

'Did you make finals this year, Grant?'

'Nah, just missed out. You?'

'Yeah, we've got the semi tomorrow.'

He had filled out as much as I'd gotten taller.

'Against who?'

'Subi.'

'Maybe I'll come and watch.'

He took a swig of his beer and looked past me. 'Okay.'

'What else have you been getting up to?' I asked.

He smiled, then. 'Still working at the shop. You know I met Gary Sobers? From the West Indies?'

'Sir Garfield Sobers?'

'Yeah, Gazza. Great bloke.'

'Unreal.'

'And I've had a few wins at the races. Spring carnival and all that.'

'Forgot you love a punt.'

'Yeah. A punt goes down a treat with the beers.'

'Don't tell Mum,' I winked.

Inside, the girls were playing with their Barbies, spread

out over the floorboards in the sitting room. Pippin was watching over them. She looked older too.

'I hear you're going to go work up north,' I said.

'That's where the work is,' she said. 'And it'll be nice to get away.'

The girls were whispering to each other, their dolls untouched on the floor.

'Look how tall the man is,' Jodee said. Peta nodded, eyes wide.

'Well, maybe I'll see you up there.'

Pippin smiled.

Mum came at me then. 'Show us your teeth!' she said, grabbing my jaw and pulling my face down to her level. I bared my teeth.

'Good, it's still in there then.'

'It's fused to the roof of my mouth, Mum.'

'Thank God for that. The amount of people who called me to tell me my son is wandering around Perth missing his front tooth. They thought you were homeless!'

I kind of was homeless.

'And you can thank Dave for paying for it.'

'Thanks, Dave!' I said, out into the ether.

'You're welcome!' he called in response, over the hood of the barbecue and through the kitchen window.

Peter was outside with one of the cousins when I grabbed him and steered him down the side of the limestone building.

'We're just going to grab smokes,' he yelled over his shoulder at a cousin, who silently waved him off.

We walked towards the store but didn't stop there. Quokkas darted under and around the picnic tables, circling our feet. Peter lifted his leg in a menacing fashion at one quokka but it didn't flinch.

'God they're annoying,' he said.

We walked past the Quod and my breath stuck in my throat. We walked south towards the old army barracks. It was windy and freezing. Down by Parakeet Bay we found a secluded toilet to shoot up in. It wasn't one of those toilets with the blue lights, thank fuck. Peter sat with his back against the door while I mixed up. We used my belt. I felt relief as soon as the dope hit. I felt every single muscle I'd been tensing at the party relax. We sat there a long time before moving to the beach. And then we just sat on the sand. Watching the lights on the yachts moored out on the ocean. Looking back at the shoreline of the Western Australian coast.

'I love looking at Perth from out here. It's so surreal,' said Peter.

'It's like a dream. Or a video game,' I said.

The grains of sand massaged my legs. The lights on the

water danced. I could hear the faint sounds of the pub in the distance. I didn't feel cold anymore.

When we got back to the police station, most people had left. Including Mum.

'She went to a lot of effort putting this on for you,' Dave said as I gathered up my bag and kissed my little sisters.

'Yeah, I'm sorry,' I said automatically.

'She's trying,' he said.

I just nodded. I didn't shake his hand.

Scott walked Peter and me to the jetty.

'Good luck tomorrow, mate,' I said, shaking his hand.

'You too,' he said.

We boarded the ferry. Peter looked at me with a face like a question mark. But I didn't say anything or correct him. I knew what he meant.

WEMBLEY

When I picked up enough coin to pay rent, I started living with Johnny in this huge old Italian mansion in Wembley, while Peter – flat broke – was back with his folks. The mansion belonged to Johnny's parents. Or it could have been his aunty's place. A big investment property on prime land, but too unwieldy for anyone to bother fixing up. There was a big wraparound wooden fence lined with agave plants which guarded the empty pool. Beyond that, steep, concrete slab steps up the hill to the two-storey house. Our bikes made the garage look huge and unnecessary. Inside everything was brown, wooden. The bathrooms had golden-yellow and spew-green tiles. Upstairs by the kitchen was a little deck where you could smell the salt of the ocean even if you couldn't see it. There were six bathrooms, impossible to keep clean. Every other house on the street was a family home. The neighbours on the beach side were a young Indian family. The neighbours on the city end had a vege patch and kept chickens.

Johnny had this real chaotic energy about him. His eyes sparkled and drew you in. You never knew what was going to come out of his mouth. He was fun. He died a couple of years ago from a brain tumour. He'd been living over East for years. We went out for one last night and we smoked a joint at the Rosemount and nearly got kicked out by security. It was so good to see him again.

When we lived together in 1979, there were guitars and band equipment all over the house. But we mostly practised in the garage. Occasionally the old bloke next door would drop by to ask us to turn it down, but he was always nice about it. Johnny and I were playing with the band at the time, so guys were always dropping in to jam. Neither of us were working, except for selling, so we were doing a lot of dope.

The closest break was City Beach. It was a bit less consistent than Cott, and it wasn't at all protected from the wind, but if you got it on the right day, it pumped. It was a different crew in the water too, guys from Scarborough I hadn't seen around before. No skinhead fuckheads. When Sam eventually got his driver's licence to get himself up there, he paddled out with me.

'Are you still going to play for Swanny this year?'

'Yeah, I suppose. Don't really know the clubs up this way.'

'We can train together.'

Sam would be playing in the first team this year, graduating from colts. I was pretty content in rezzies, not that I had a chance in the league team anyway.

'Sounds good, mate.'

The house at Wembley was almost the inverse of Marine Parade, where instead of absorbing the outside elements, it was a completely different world inside. The tiled floors made it cool all the time, and the walls were bricked and heavy, so it was hard to tell what was happening in the outside world. Especially from the ground floor, which jutted against the hillside and so had no windows on the south wall. It was the same as Marine Parade in that there were always people over, though. But I didn't really mind.

The band had our first gig at the house. We set up in the empty pool – the shape of the concrete bowl made the sound reverberate so much you couldn't tell which way the music was coming from. It was incredible. It was warm too. We could have stayed there all night. But the girls had to keep traversing the stairs to use the toilet. And as the night wore on, they became ever more treacherous. When Debbie stacked it halfway up, safely landing in the bushes but scraping her knees to the bone, we moved the party inside.

***

In March, Ralphy's stash finally ran out. I remember it was March because it was around Pippin's birthday. At first I barely noticed. Johnny and I had built up a vast network of suppliers among our musician and surfer mates. It made it fun really, waking up and brainstorming where to go to score. Once we scored from some Italian guys in the back of a pool room in Northbridge. Another time we scored at a Rockets concert. The dope was stronger shit too. But it was more expensive and without any other income than the dole, money was tight.

We were spending a lot of time in the house. Sometimes I'd all of a sudden become aware that it'd been days since I'd left. Or even went outside. Especially when it was cold and the breeze whipped up against the balcony. When the weather was good, it was enough to just roam around the huge garden, picking up weeds, running my hands over the agave plants. Sometimes I'd just sit on the edge of the empty pool, swinging my legs back and forth. For hours.

It was two days before our dole cheques came and there was no food in the house, save for some spices on the spice rack. We were out on the deck surveying the city, smoking our last cigarettes when Johnny said, 'Could eat, hey.'

'Same,' I said.

The lights from the city skyline twinkled. It was still. A soft *buck-buck-buck* floated over from the city side neighbour's chook pen. Johnny looked me dead in the eye.

'You want me to steal a chicken,' Johnny said.

'Fuck, how'd you know?'

'Because the last meal we had, we ate together. Two days ago. And it was toast.'

We were laughing but he was serious.

'They have so many anyway, they won't even notice one's gone,' I said.

'Fuck it,' he said, standing up.

'I'll preheat the oven.'

Johnny made his way down the front hill and jumped over the asbestos fence that flanked the pool to the city side neighbour's backyard. I was conscious of the sound of his footsteps in the grass. But no one stirred. The dog must have been inside. I could hear the chickens *buck-buck-bucking.* I could hear the creak of a gate swinging open and the brush of a body against chicken wire. I imagined I could hear footsteps on the hay in the little barn shed. *Buuurrrrrrrrck*, one of the hens said. Johnny chucked the hen over the fence. She seemed pretty calm so I decided to pick her up. She clipped at my hand with her beak but didn't flap or squirm or anything. Johnny hiked himself over after her and I assisted in sliding him down, before buckling in half, laughing. She was picking at the grass by his feet, unperturbed.

'Shut the fuck up,' Johnny said.

The light was already on in the garden shed. I don't think I'd even been in there up until that point. It was just a dusty work bench with old rusty tools hanging on the wall behind it. And buckets and tubs of crap.

'I have to confess, I haven't planned this far ahead,' I said.

'Just hold her still,' Johnny said, searching. I found an axe by a pile of firewood.

'Remember that for winter,' Johnny said. His voice was light but his eyes betrayed him.

Johnny shrugged and swung the axe down on the hen's neck. Her head popped clean right off. It happened so quickly that it took me a while to register it – I was still holding her headless body down.

'Come on, mate,' Johnny said.

The worst part was definitely the plucking. We put her in the sink and stood there for nearly an hour ripping the feathers out of her dead skin. I had to sit it out for a while. I thought I was going to spew. When she was naked, Johnny lashed her with oil and rubbed some rosemary on her. We didn't have anything for stuffing so he shoved an Export can up there. We let her cook.

When Johnny pulled her out, he carved her up silently, dishing a wing and a leg on to each of our plates. He was so sombre I thought he might suggest saying a prayer. We chewed in silence.

'This is, without a doubt, the driest roast chicken I've ever had.'

I picked the stringy chicken bits from my teeth.

'Poor hen,' Johnny said.

***

The Rockets were playing at the Albion with the Suspects. At the bar after the set, I bumped into Charlie.

'Back from Sydney?' I asked.

'For now,' he said. He looked me up and down. 'Are you looking to score?'

I'd never spoken to him about dope before. It must have been written on my face.

'Actually yeah,' I said.

'Come to my place, there's some you should try.'

I followed him on the Thunderbird again. He was on his bike this time. Susie wasn't home, and for some reason I was thankful. I didn't want her to see me shooting up, I guess.

He had a little chemistry set-up in his office. All the dope was sectioned off into little packets that looked like water balloons. Or little plastic parachutes.

'This is new. From Malaysia,' he said, mixing the dope in a little ceramic bowl and withdrawing the brown liquid into a syringe.

'Aren't you having any?' I asked as I tied the belt tight around my arm.

'No,' he said. 'Let me know what you think.'

He injected the brown liquid into the underside of my arm.

I sank into myself.

When I gathered myself together Charlie was in the lounge room.

'That good?' he asked.

I just smiled.

'I can give you a couple of grams for your friends, just pay me back when you get the cash.'

I smiled again.

That weekend The Riffs were playing at Steves. I shifted the bags Charlie had given me, making sure to leave some aside for Johnny and me. I don't think The Riffs had even started their second set when I'd already run dry. Even their drummer was enquiring after my services.

It's kind of hard to piece everything together at this point. As I said, the house at Wembley was kind of a wormhole. And we were doing a lot of dope. There are some months that I just don't remember. I hope my family didn't see me at that stage in my life. It's hard not to be embarrassed, ashamed about it.

***

That year Swanny had gotten into the finals. I'd missed a few games and training sessions because I couldn't afford to put fuel in the Thunderbird, but I'd been playing steadily in the lead-up. We flogged Mosman Park in the quarter final where I roved around the ground. The semi was closer – against Subi. I played in the forward line the whole game. Kicked three goals. And we ended up winning by two.

We had a couple of beers after the game at the Swanny Hotel. I bumped into a few of the guys from Steves.

'Mate, where did you get that dope from?' a few of them said.

'I've never had anything like that.'

It really had put Ralphy's stash to shame.

'I'll let you know when I pick up some more,' I said.

I don't know when it happened really but all of a sudden everyone was on dope. Or I only ever saw people who were also on dope. It's hard to distinguish between those two possibilities. But it was rife. I don't think people really know that about Perth. These days there's a moral panic about meth. But I just don't remember the media having any interest in the heroin scene back then. I wasn't really reading the paper, though, in 1979.

On Saturday 22 September, the Swanbourne Swans played Scarborough in the reserves grand final. I played centre half-forward for the whole match. And it was close. Scarborough had obviously stacked their side with A-Grade players. We even recognised some West Australian Football League players in their team. All was fair in love and war, I supposed. But we had no such luck because our A-Grade league side was playing their grand final that same afternoon. They held us to just four goals in the first half. We held them to five. The rover they had on me was ruthless – I barely got a touch before the siren sounded at half-time. Coach went psycho at the huddle.

'You lazy pieces of shit,' he started, glaring at every one

of us. 'Don't just settle in with the bloke on your mark. Break away from them for fuck's sake. You boys up front need to be able to outrun them.'

'They've got Tigers rookies out there, Coach,' Johnny said.

'I don't give a rat's arse!' he barked. 'Outrun them. Get to the ball first!'

It started to sprinkle as we took the ground for the third quarter.

'Still here?' said my opponent as I caught up with him at the fifty-metre line. 'Thought you'd be out hitting the needle by now. Or is that what you blokes use in lieu of oranges at half-time.'

I felt heat creep up the back of my neck but I didn't say anything. The siren blew, and then the umpire's whistle. The ball went straight to our backline, a rushed behind, and back again to the wing. The stalemate unbroken. Until Johnny switched the ball to the opposing wing out of the blue, catching both me and my opponent off-guard.

Outrun him.

Get to the ball first.

I ran wide, dangerously close to the boundary line, outstretched my left hand and landed the mark. Straight away I dropped the ball to my boot and kicked it into the goal square. Peter marked it. Then kicked it straight through the goals. And then we were tied. Five goals, four points apiece. The siren wailed. I can't really remember what Coach said to us at three-quarter time, other than hurling abuse. I was running on pure adrenaline at that point.

In the fourth, the ruckmen tussled and tapped the ball out. It bounced our way, then theirs. One of us would score, and then the other. Like points following serve at a tennis match. Until the scores were eight goals six apiece. Forty-five points. My opponent hadn't piped up in a while. His smirk had morphed into more of a grimace. The ground was slippery now. It was harder to keep your feet. It was surely nearing the end. I strained my eyes at the dugout, but no one was offering any sign of the time. The ball was in our back fifty. And then through the centre. And our forward fifty when one of the Scarborough guys clotheslined Johnny right on the fifty-metre line. The crowd let out a groan. The siren wailed. The umpire gave Johnny a free kick. I couldn't even watch. I felt sick for the bloke. No one expected him to kick it under the pressure. That far out. In the rain.

We watched the ball soar toward the goals.

Screams rang in my ears.

The crowd jumped the boundary fence and rushed the ground.

We drank at the Cott Hotel all afternoon, singing and chanting, pouring pints over each other's heads. We were euphoric. Pope was there too, singing along with us, one hand in salute. Sam and the league team came down midafternoon. They didn't win but were drinking as if they had.

As the sun went down, I went to Charlie's. Susie was making tea – roast lamb.

'Well done on the premiership! I'm proud of you,' she said as I entered the kitchen, hugging me and kissing me on the cheek.

'Thanks, Sue,' I said.

She cracked open a beer for me.

Charlie was in his office. He had little piles of little plastic bags of little parachutes of the dope, all sectioned out for me. I handed him the money that I owed in cash. He silently handed back two fifties.

'This is that Malaysian gear that you tried.'

'It was popular.'

'That's good to hear.' He gathered the bags in the bags all together in a paper bag and handed it over. I shoved it into my backpack.

'There's more here this time, it should keep you going for a while,' he said. 'You should be able to have some money at the end too. To get by.'

I nodded. I didn't know how else to express my gratitude. He smiled and clapped me on the arm.

'Look after yourself, though,' he said.

I've thought about Charlie and Susie a lot, since. What was it I loved about them? I think I loved how much they loved each other. They were like surrogate parents to me, even though we were roughly the same age. They were a team, strong. There was something comforting in that for me. And I'd never felt like that before.

Charlie carved the roast. Susie had set the dining table immaculately. She fussed around while Charlie dished up the lamb with his carving knife and fork, filling our glasses with wine, dropping bread rolls on our side tables, doling out potatoes and peas, passing around the gravy boat. When she finally sat down, she grabbed my hand tight.

'I'm so proud of you,' she said. 'Our winner!'

AN EK PARKED ON HAWKSTONE STREET

Johnny's aunty or parents or whatever were selling up the Wembley house, so we got kicked out. I didn't have any money for a bond for a rental. So for a while I was living out of my 1961 Holden EK. I still had the Thunderbird – tucked away in Michael's parents' garage in Swanbourne – while I parked the EK out front of Simsy's house on Hawkstone Street in Cottesloe. Simsy was your classic middle-to-upper class vagabond who dressed like a homeless person and talked socialist politics like he'd grown up poor, when in actual fact he'd attended one of the most prestigious boys schools in the state.

The shade from the bottlebrushes and breeze from the ocean made it comfortable enough. And the bench seats did alright.

I wasn't sleeping much anyway. Simsy's place was an old heritage cottage build – burgundy and off-white with a steep, pointed roof that had a little castle turret in the centre, complete with stained-glass windows and a white picket fence. A British colonial architectural hangover. The garden was bare but for an orange tree. The rest of the street bore roses and lavender and BMWs in limestone driveways. Looking west, you could see the patch of blue of the ocean flanked by the Norfolk pines at Cott Beach. You could even see Rotto from the hood of the EK on a clear day. Facing east, looking down over the hill, you could see busy Stirling Highway and the railway tracks of the defunct Fremantle Line, unused since Premier Charlie Court decommissioned it the year before. From that vantage point, Cottesloe was my kingdom. Even if I had to knock on Simsy's door to request a shower or a shit.

In the Cottesloe scene, demand for dope was steadily increasing. Charlie's Malaysian gear was hot. I nearly couldn't head out to a party or a gig without it. One night we were at the North Cott Surf Lifesaving Club checking out the Rockets, and I unloaded maybe five hundred dollars' worth before the band even started. I had to call Charlie from the bar to meet me at the hamburger joint, Eats on the Beach, with more gear during the break.

'Got your licence yet?' he asked, motioning at the Thunderbird.

'Working on it,' I lied. I tore the paper off my hamburger. It was a bit soggy. Dripping with fat. I took a big bite, catching a little corner of the paper in my mouth. I forgot to ask for no beetroot.

Charlie laughed. 'Look, you're shifting this stuff pretty quickly. You might want to lean on your networks to ensure there's healthy supply elsewhere. Just in case of any disruptions.'

I wondered if he could tell how reliant I'd become on it just by looking at me. Probably.

'Roger that.'

I picked up some plastic buckets off the back of a truck, so to speak. And would bring them in the shower with me, fill them up with the shower water, and use them to wash my clothes. I had a bar of Imperial Leather soap and that seemed to do the trick. I'd hang them over Simsy's picket fence to dry or on the dash of the EK if it threatened to rain.

On Fridays we'd go to the Regal Theatre to watch surf movies. But I was finding it harder and harder to scrape the money together to buy a ticket. Sometimes I'd sneak in by going to the toilet first and then doubling back after the attendant had already checked everyone else's tickets. The water looked unreal on the big screen in colour. Outside in Subiaco everything was painted burgundy and stained red by bore water. The streets were always packed with people. So much so that it was impossible to go out and not bump into someone – friend or relative. I was always seeing my cousins or the old crew from Hollywood on Rokeby Road. In addition to the people looking to score.

Sometimes I'd think about the family. Mum. Dave. Pippin. Scott. Jodee. Peta. They were so close. Soon they'd be living in Cottesloe themselves, not far from where I was, living out of my car. But I hadn't seen them in years. My heart aches when I think about the person I was then – how ashamed. I want to wrap my arms around him. And tell him it's not his fault.

I didn't realise until the footy season started that I'd completely missed preseason training. I'm sure Peter or Sam would have told me about it. My stomach turned at the thought of facing Coach's wrath. So when I heard the first game was scheduled for early April, I just didn't rock up. In hindsight I probably couldn't have afforded the registration fees anyway.

Everything had become about scoring. I had taken Charlie's advice and diversified our heroin supply chain. Michael had a guy. Simsy had a guy. Johnny had a guy. I had Charlie. Spreading the risk. Future-proofing. Almost every day we woke up and conferred in Simsy's lounge room, calling our networks and establishing a pick-up plan.

The morning was set aside for quality assurance (sampling the product). And occasionally the nights were set aside too (distribution). Followed by write-offs of whatever stock was left over at the end of the day. It was a well-oiled scoring machine. But whatever money I had been making with Charlie's gear was now almost immediately tied up in the next day's stash. I was nowhere closer to a bond deposit than I had been six months earlier.

It was oddly quiet on Hawkstone Street. Eerie even. Maybe because it was so perfect. It was impossible to feel relaxed. It may sound like that could have something to do with my sleeping in my car but, honestly, I could sleep anywhere. It was the vibe. An insular, golden-triangle soccer-mum nightmare.

In winter Sam and I went out for a paddle. The main break was clear of surf lifesavers so we met there. It was cold enough for me to notice the hole forming in the leg of my wetsuit. But there was no wind and the sun was out. I hadn't seen Sam since grand final day.

'Are you still tiling floors?'

'Nah, I haven't done that for a few months now. Maybe a year.'

'Oh yeah.'

The swell was pretty average. Sam rode a few small

barrels to the shore while we were out there, but I didn't really have the energy. I wound up just floating on my board, lightly paddling with my feet.

'What are you doing now?'

'I've started my apprenticeship. Plumbing.'

'That's great, mate. Always a job in plumbing.'

'We miss you at footy.'

'Yeah?'

We didn't stay out too long, though long enough for my hole to become a sizable tear. On the shore we gathered our things and had a rinse at the showers. Sam started telling me about a stand-off with a local Aboriginal mob up north, the unions and a mining company. Noonkanbah.

'Honestly mate, it's been going on for years. The mob don't want anyone drilling there because it's sacred land. But Charlie Court doesn't give a shit. He's just egging the miners on.'

'That's unreal.'

'Yeah, up near Fitzroy Crossing, the mob are literally out there blocking the path of the diggers!'

It was quiet up at the Cott Hotel. Just a couple of old codgers at the front bar. No Pope. The clock still safely secured on the wall, however. The old codgers were sitting either side of a wireless, their necks craned, listening to the cricket. Australia was playing the West Indies. Their hushed tones seemed to indicate we weren't doing well. Sam and I didn't even bother staying for a feed. We just necked our middies and left for Hawkstone Street.

'Heard Pippin's going well up north,' Sam said, gathering his bag.

'Yeah?'

'A lot of work there, hey. Couple of breaks too, I think.'

'I haven't spoken to her,' I said.

It was gusty out on Marine Parade. I was shivering in my jumper.

'Are your folks still at Rotto?' Sam asked.

'Yeah, I think so.'

'We should head over for a surf again. Could crash at theirs.'

'Yeah.'

By the time we got to Hawkstone Street we were at a trot just to warm ourselves up.

That night Sam and I snuck in to see a movie at the Lakeway Drive-In in Swanbourne. We jumped the back fence and sat on the back of the hill, turning the little speaker up so we could hear it back where we sat in darkness. We had gone there on a whim so had no idea what was showing. The previews finished and the lights came down. The film started with a wide, open, mountainous landscape. A lake with an island in the middle. A winding road flanked by pine trees with a lonesome car driving along it. Blue mountains. Foreboding bass. Blue sky. Violin. Grey mountains. The car is a yellow beetle. Big, bold, capital letters enter the frame.

A STANLEY KUBRICK FILM

'Ah Jesus,' whispered Sam.

THE SHINING

I noticed the woman on screen was reading *The Catcher in the Rye*. Even with the sound dulled by the distance between us and the speaker and the open air, the piercing sounds of wind and screeching violins had me terrified. The little boy looked like Scott. When the ghost butler man said the word 'nigger', I felt my face flush hot.

We were silent on the walk home. I felt sick in the stomach. Too scared to open my mouth for fear of spewing. It felt like the time I was on the ride at the Royal Show with the chairs on chains that swing around and around, too scared to scream.

'Fucking bad vibes in that hotel,' Sam eventually said. 'Shouldn't have built it on those Indian graves.'

'Yeah, like Rotto.'

Sam laughed. 'Fuck oath. Like Rotto.'

When we turned into Hawkstone Street there was a cop car parked in Simsy's driveway. Dave was leaning against the passenger side door – in plainclothes – his head through the open window. There was another copper in the driver's seat. He must have seen me coming through the side mirror because Dave whirled around to look at me.

'Get in the car,' he said.

'What's going on?' I asked, looking from Dave to Sam in a sort of plea for help. Sam shrugged. I sat in the back seat of the car. Leather seats again.

'Thanks, Dick, mate. Just to Charlie Gairdner's please,' Dave said to the copper. 'Your brother has been in a car accident,' he said to me.

I don't know if I managed a word in response.

Scott was propped up on a mound of pillows on the hospital bed. His eyes black. Nose taped. Mum had already left, apparently. Dave sat down in the chair by the toilet door. I sat on the edge of the bed. Scott looked so vulnerable, against the baby-blue backdrop of the privacy curtain.

'What happened?'

'Ploughed into a wall on Eric Street.'

'Drunk?'

'Yep.' He had a sheepish grin on his face. Dave didn't say a word. I felt guilty, I'm not sure why.

'Well, we can't have that, can we? You're the dependable one. Disappointing Mum is my job.'

He laughed and winced.

‘How’s the car?’

‘Written off.’

‘Ah well. Dave might buy you one for your twenty-first.’ I winked. Dave grunted. Scott smiled.

That night I went to see Susie and Charlie. I noticed my hands were still shaking when Susie handed me a glass of red. Maybe they hadn’t stopped shaking since the drive-in.

‘Your poor brother. Charlie came off his bike in Nepal and it shook us both up,’ she said, looking up at him.

‘I’m a lot more careful now,’ he said, massaging her shoulder.

‘I guess I’m still in shock.’

Susie draped a blanket over my legs. I hadn’t even noticed I was shivering. It was so quiet that I could hear waves crashing faintly in the background.

‘I’m going back over to Sydney in the new year. Not sure how long for,’ Charlie said. ‘Looking to set up a business, maybe.’ He looked up at Susie, smiling.

‘And I’ve got family over East,’ Susie said.

‘Okay, I hope you’re not gone too long,’ I said.

‘You’ll manage,’ said Charlie.

***

I was sleeping in the EK when I heard a tapping on the windscreen. It was the goddamn cop who drove us to the hospital. I wound down the window.

'G'day, Dick,' I said. I realised I'd met him a couple of times before, at a barbecue or something Mum and Dave had put on for their friends. Dick was bald with a moustache and the air of an arsehole. Like if someone asked you to conjure up an image of a pig copper, it'd be Dick.

'Look, you're going to have to move on from here. There's been some complaints,' he said, motioning to Hawkstone Street at large.

'Of course. It's only temporary.'

'It doesn't look temporary.' He cocked his eyebrow at the mountain of clothes on the passenger seat.

'Yep, noted, sir. I'll sort it out.'

'Now you've got a good family, son. I don't want to have to pick you up again, understand?'

Then Dick left. I was a bit rattled and I didn't want to go back to sleep. So I got out of the EK and wandered down the hill towards Stirling Highway. I walked all the way down the street lined with bottlebrushes, stars barely visible between them. At the railway I automatically looked each way for a train. Muscle memory. When I realised my mistake, I stepped onto the tracks and just stood there for a while. I remembered Scott's face when I nearly died at Shenton Park train station that time. I felt the urge to sit cross-legged on the tracks, but I didn't. I just stood there. Until after a while I started walking again. Vaguely towards the river.

The Swan was the same as always. It comforted me, the brown, murky water. The street lamps and lights from the city and the stars reflected in the blackness of the water. I thought about the sharks – still there. Feeding on the jellyfish and rats. Stronger – now. Threatening to cross the jetty threshold onto land and swallow me whole.

It was midway through 1980 when Robert finally got kicked out of The Suspects. We were sitting in Simsy's lounge room when the phone rang. Simsy ran to the kitchen to answer it, before returning to the lounge room.

'Rob, it's for you.'

Robert wore a sheepish grin when he returned. 'It finally happened. The Suspects don't want me back.'

We all cracked up.

'Well, you're the last man standing then Micky' said Simsy.

Michael cocked an eyebrow. 'For now!'

CORNWALL STREET

The last place I moved into – before everything that came next – was Michael's place on Cornwall Street, just off Servetus Street in Swanbourne. It was a tight street on a hill full of bottlebrushes. There was a little park at the end of the road with eucalyptus trees and cricket nets. It was shady and the road was stained with brown leaves like Lyall Street. It reminded me of Scott. The house was a plain sixties build with cream carpets. It was Michael's family home but everyone else had left. The next-door neighbours must have been friends with Bob Hawke, who'd been the national president of the ACTU, because Michael said he'd seen him there a couple of times.

It was one of those rare weather events in Perth where it hadn't stopped raining for a couple of weeks. It was just grey all of the time and the rain was relentless. Not overly heavy, but constant, and it sapped the joy out of everyone. Not that any of us on the gear had truly felt joy for a while, but everyone was irritable and bickering, constantly. It just felt like the end.

It was on a Tuesday that Brett came over to tell us Ralphy had overdosed. I felt so sad that I was sick. Ralphy had lived a hard life. Don't get me wrong, he was an absolute piece of shit. But witnessing your dad kill your mum then turn the gun on himself would turn anyone rotten, wouldn't it?

'Any idea whose dope it was?' asked Michael.

Brett shook his head.

'I don't think it matters, it can happen with any stash if you shoot too much.'

'With Ralphy, and Jen last month ...' Brett held up his thumb and index finger, 'plus James, Rob, Debbie, Macca and Fi ...' His palms were facing up and he was looking down at the seven fingers he'd counted out. Each one signifying a friend of ours who had OD'd on heroin. 'In the past eighteen months.'

'Jesus,' said Michael.

I couldn't believe it had taken two hands. It didn't feel real. It felt like I was looking at myself from outside of myself – completely detached. Unable to draw any connection between Brett staring at his hands and Michael mixing up another bag. I just quietly played my part and tied a belt around my arm.

It's funny how you get desensitised to death. It should come as no surprise, I suppose, that drug addicts would be numb to grief as much as they are to the many other emotions they've stunted from years of substance abuse. But for years after, I struggled to cry. Like I was scared to let the pain or grief in, lest it overcome me. Some people spend their whole lives like this.

At some point – it may have been June or July because I'm pretty sure the Australian cricket team was in England for The Ashes – Michael's contacts had run dry. I'd tried calling Charlie but no one was answering. Not even Susie. So I went over anyway. I probably beat on the door for four minutes before Susie finally answered it.

'He's not here, darling,' she said.

'When will he be back?'

'Not for a while. He's back in Sydney.'

My hands were red raw from slapping them against the wooden door.

'Did he leave anything for me?'

She looked at me with such pity that I felt my face flush and eyes water.

'I'm sorry, Grant.'

I expected Michael or Brett or someone else to have picked up some dope by the time I got home. But no one was there. I was sweating. I immediately threw my jumper off and went into the kitchen to splash some water on my face. There was no note – no clue where they'd gone. I felt nauseous so I sat down. I felt cold so I put my jumper back on and rested my head against the wall. I could feel sweat pooling under my knees and dripping down my spine.

I felt liquid pooling in my mouth and knew I was going to spew, so I ran for the toilet. I had one foot in the cubicle when I started spewing. Then I got the shits. There wasn't a bin in the cubicle so when I started spewing again, I tried to aim between my legs straight into the bowl but I dribbled vomit all over my jumper. I passed out. I had that nightmare where the little gremlins lifted up my bed and carried me away. When I woke up, I heard someone coming through the front door. I crawled to the lounge room.

'Jesus, mate, what happened to you?' asked Michael, dropping to the floor to sit by me, cross-legged. He immediately started mixing up the dope. I couldn't even speak. I just lay spread-eagled on my back and let him tie up my arm for me.

***

I missed Scott. I'd heard he was real into indoor cricket now, though I battled to envision how one would play cricket indoors. I wanted to speak to him. But I didn't even know where to reach him. I assumed he'd moved out of the police station at Rotto, but I wasn't sure. And I didn't want to call Mum to find out.

In those days I thought about Scott all the time. And I felt guilty, because I felt responsible for him. It's probably how most siblings feel when they grow up in a dysfunctional family, right? That you just want to protect them at all costs. That they are the only ones who know everything, who've been through every significant event and trauma that you have. They know the whole you. For some reason I didn't worry about Pippin. She was so strong. But I worried about Scott.

Sam had tried calling a few times and had left messages with Michael, but I hadn't called him back. At some point he just came around. It must have been on a weekend because he was working full-time.

'Mate, let's go surf the main break. It's pumping,' Sam said.

I was keen for a paddle, but I knew Michael would be

back with a stash and I didn't want to leave it too late, else risk missing out.

'Nah, not today, man.'

'We're well overdue.'

'Yeah, I know. How's footy?'

'Yeah, it's alright – second on the ladder. What's that?' He was frowning, looking at my face, mouth.

'Cold sore or something.'

'There's another one on your neck.'

I rubbed my hand over the skin on my neck. I couldn't feel anything.

'Look, man, don't let me keep you. I'll come out next time.'

'Yeah, alright,' he said. He was still frowning. Even hours after he'd left, I couldn't get out of my head the image of him frowning at my mouth.

In August the rain finally broke. But it was still colder than usual. And though the sun was shining, the overwhelming sense of dread remained. It was like a Hitchcock film, where the camera pans to the bomb under the table and back up to the people's faces. It was not a matter of *if* it was all going to blow but, rather, when.

One day Charlie came over. I had my *Exile on Main St.* record on, and I was just playing along on my Gibson SG.

Charlie was smoking a cigarette and sitting deep in the hinge of the couch. He told me all about Sydney and his plans to move him and Susie over there for good.

'Isn't it cold over East?' I asked.

'A little bit.'

I didn't say anything to that, just kept playing along to the record.

'You'll understand when you get married.'

I couldn't imagine that I would.

***

It was strange. I knew it was September because the footy finals were on. And my birthday came and went. But I didn't feel that warm afternoon air, the smell of the native flowers or the salt in the air, like normal. It was still too cold. No Royal Show weather this year.

'Grant, come here. Now.' Michael was calling from the front room. His voice was shaking. My heart leaped into my throat. I walked in to see him looking out the window, his head under the beige, sun-bleached curtain, facing the road. My stomach dropped.

'Who is it?'

I was suddenly aware of my breath. I had to consciously tell myself to breathe in and breathe out. Shaking, I pulled the curtain to the side to look out. There was a black car parked out the front, with two men in dark suits standing either side. They looked like detectives or something.

'Are those guns?' I asked, straining my eyes at their belts. I imagined they were wearing bulletproof vests. I thought I was going to throw up.

'Oh my god!' Michael shouted. I cowered, lifting my arms in front of my face like I was shielding it from a cricket ball.

'What?'

Michael was pointing to our right, his fingertip smudged against the window. A bloke with silver hair and a long stride was walking out of the house and towards the car with the men in the suits.

'It's Bob Hawke!'

'Fuck off.'

The man strode towards the car, turning to wave at the neighbour standing on his porch before sliding into the back seat. It was Bob Hawke. Michael gave a silent salute. I felt my body relax.

I missed Sam's twenty-first birthday. I didn't forget about it, per se. The party I mean. When it came around, I was in no fit state to ride the Thunderbird, the EK had a canary – a yellow sticker deeming it unroadworthy – and I had no money for the cab fare. Also the sore on my neck had sort of spread down my chest and I couldn't get Sam's frown out of my head still, so I didn't want to go and see him again in the flesh, worrying about me. Or see all the old footy boys. I was too aware of how skinny I was. I didn't even call Sam to tell him. I just pushed the frown and the worry and the guilt to the shadow realm of myself with all the other unpleasantness and got high with Michael and Johnny and whoever else came over that night.

The house was a tip. Neither Michael nor I had cleaned since we moved in. I saw a mouse a couple of times, darting between the couches and behind the amps set up in the front room. Michael talked about going to Woolies to pick up a mousetrap, but he never did. I didn't really mind the little guy anyway. Except for the time I was lying on the couch, eating from the salt and vinegar chips packet I'd just found on the floor, when my hand went through the bottom of the packet, which the mouse had clearly chewed through. The thought of the little guy running all over the chips, nibbling on them, then me having a go at them turned my stomach. The little shit.

One afternoon, Lois rang. I supposed Robert or Darcy gave her the number at Cornwall to reach me. I hadn't spoken to her since I moved out.

'Grant, your mail is still coming to the shop, love.'

'Sorry about that.'

'It's okay it's not a problem.' She paused. She sort of had a scratch in her throat. Croaky. 'It's just that there seem to be some unpaid bills or something. Most are from the Department of Transport.'

'Oh, okay.'

'Why don't you come by and pick them up? It'd be good to see you.'

'Yeah. Okay, Lois. Bye.'

'Bye, love.'

Fuck that. I was determined to stay blissfully ignorant of whatever the fuck was in those envelopes. It was nice to hear from Lois, though. I needed a cigarette. I opened the pack on the kitchen bench by the phone to help myself, but it was empty. I went into Michael's room to check the pack that usually resided on his bedside table, but that was gone, with him presumably. I even checked the emergency packet in my leather jacket's back pocket. Nothing. Instead, I sat down in the middle of the lounge room and started mixing up the dope. I tied the belt around my arm.

I was in the outhouse at Ga and Jempa's place. There were spider webs hanging on the walls and the roof. A spider crawled over the door handle. I wanted to wee but I couldn't. It was cold. And I couldn't pull my pants back up because they had dropped to the floor and I couldn't reach them. And they were covered in spider webs. There was a banging on the door and a squeal, and it shook the spider on its web. So much so that it dropped down about an inch and I froze. But the spider steadied himself and climbed back up his web to perch on the door handle once again.

It must have been the next morning. I had fallen asleep in the lounge. The front door flew open, half coming off its hinges. And then the house was filled with police with arms outstretched, eyes squinted, looking through the sights of their guns. I can't remember what they said exactly – they were yelling. If they had a warrant – I've thought about this a lot – they didn't show it. I put my hands behind my head and a cop tightened handcuffs over my wrists. I saw Michael being led out of his room in cuffs too. He didn't even look up at me. They put us in separate paddy wagons. I looked through the cage that separated me from the driver and could tell by the eyes in the rear-view mirror that the copper was Dick. Dave's mate. It may as well have been Dave driving the paddy wagon. I sat back into the leather seat and closed my eyes.

'Alright, you've been found with ten grams of heroin.'

At least I think that's how much it was. Isn't it insane

that I don't remember? We were in a little white room with two desks pushed together, a water fountain and one of those pedestal fans that make your voice sound funny when you sing up close into them. It wasn't Dick interrogating me but a younger man in a suit. He looked like a detective, I guess. Dick just sat there quietly. Staring at me. He quoted the street value at me. I can't remember what it was.

'That's a bit more than personal use, isn't it?' he said.

I couldn't tell if the question was rhetorical or not so I shrugged in response. The detective frowned.

'This is serious, mate. Take this seriously.'

'I am.'

If I'd known I could have had a lawyer advising me at that point, and if I could have afforded a lawyer, I wouldn't have said anything further. If I'd known I had a right to remain silent then I would have exercised that right. But I didn't know.

The detective stood up and walked over to the water fountain. He quietly filled up two styrofoam cups and put them down in front of himself and Dick. All of a sudden, I was aware of how dry my mouth was. My tongue felt heavy. I had to consciously swallow my own spit. The sound reverberated in my ears.

'Was it for personal use or did you sell it on?' asked the detective.

'Well, it was personal, but sometimes I'd pass some on to friends and that.'

'Sell it on to others?'

'Just to friends, at parties or whatever. We'd all take turns scoring, you know?'

His face was frozen in this condescending baby frown. Dick was deadpan.

'So you were distributing it. What involvement did Michael have?'

I shook my head at that. I wasn't about to get Michael in the shit. His family would be distraught. I took another conscious swallow.

'Come on, what was Michael's role in the distribution network?' the detective asked again.

I was so confused.

'Who is your supplier?'

There was no way I was going to say it was Charlie.

'I don't know.'

'Bullshit.' Dick slammed his fist against the desk. The image of Dave turning snags on the barbecue flooded my brain. I wanted to cry. I swallowed, hard.

'Look, you're in a world of shit. You've been caught dealing heroin. We know you're a pissant middleman. If you don't give us any more information about those higher up the chain then we can't help you.'

'I'm not a dealer,' I said.

I don't know if they heard me.

I think Dave bailed me out. I don't remember.

I was in there now. In the river. Completely submerged. My head under the brown, murky water. I trod water, swinging and batting my hands around in front of me, searching. There was nothing there. I was alone.

My case was heard at the District Court in Perth. I had to sell my Gibson SG guitar and Triumph Thunderbird motorbike to pay for a lawyer for the trial. After the evidence was heard I'd given up in my police interview, I was sentenced to four years with a sixteen-month minimum. 'Sold heroin.' That's all it said regarding the charge on my prisoner identification card. Two words, followed by another three. 'No fixed address.'

FREMANTLE PRISON

Fremantle Prison was a limestone fortress built by convicts for convicts in the 1850s. And it had remained largely unchanged since then. I shit you not. When I got locked up, our cells were still the same draconian, colonial torture boxes. There was barely clean running water. No insulation to maintain warmth and certainly no heating in the winter. It stank of shit and death. This of course being the place where the last man in Western Australia was hanged. Mum always told that story – that she only got a job at the Charles Hotel because the barmaid before her had been shot by Cooke, right in the arm, so she was no longer able to pull a pint. I hated sharing quarters with that particular ghost. At night I imagined I could hear his screams. I heard the whoosh of the drop and the thumping sound of the noose. I heard wet footsteps with no body. I heard the scratching of rats against the concrete and imagined them crawling all over my skin.

When I went in in 1981, they put me in Main Division with the hard crooks. I shared a cell with this bloke Russell, who I knew from Mount Claremont. He'd gotten drunk and bashed and raped a woman at a party. He was a bit of an arsehole. He mostly left me alone, though. Old Jack was in there too. I knew him from Cott, a mate of Pope's – he'd been conscripted as a medic in the Vietnam War. Sent him a bit nutty. He was a good mate to me, always happy to sit and have a chat about the war, or shit on Charlie Court.

I worked in the tailor shop to start with, making prison uniforms. Some of the career criminals liked their uniforms custom made. So I'd take their designs and fit it how they liked it in exchange for a packet of cigarettes. One of my valued customers was the notorious Archie Butterly.

He'd attempted an escape by digging a hole in the wall of his cell a year earlier. He and another bloke dug their way through the chapel and removed bars out of a window and everything. But he fell down a couple of floors and broke his foot in the process. So he turned himself in. He was in for robbing a bank and killing a guy or something. Anyway, I built up a bit of a friendship with him, tailoring his clothes. Turns out he was not simply dealing in cigarettes – the currency of choice at Freo – he was also the bookie. He had so many packets that he had to store some of them in other blokes' cells, lest the guards confiscate them. The quota was seven packs per cell. So I'd get a pack per week for hoarding some for him, and when he needed to top up we'd meet in the yard and I'd hand it over. It was a pretty good deal.

They let us pick classes, run through the university or whatever, so I decided to study English. I hadn't ever really read until then. The education officer was this American guy called Bud. He was a nice guy. Full of energy and goodwill. Real American. He got me to read *The Catcher in the Rye*. Honestly, he was probably the only person who worked at the prison who wasn't an arsehole to the Aboriginal guys. Archie studied English too. He was real into poetry.

I know now that it's common for drug addicts who end up in prison to continue using. That in prison it's ubiquitous. And I'm sure that was the case at Fremantle too. I don't really remember making a conscious choice to stop. It wasn't like a switch turned off in my head or anything like that, I just didn't seek it out while I was inside. I can't say I didn't ever try it again. Any drug addict will tell you relapses are inevitable. And it's embarrassing as hell. But they were few and far between.

Towards the end of winter, Robert wrote to tell me that Lois had died. Cancer. 'Loi X'd it.' That's how he broke the news. A simple addendum at the end of his letter.

Not long after that, Bud moved me out of the tailor shop

to the library. I'd potter away, putting aside piles of books I planned to read myself as well as recommendations for Old Jack. I'd bring my acoustic guitar in and run workshops, teaching the other blokes how to play.

Prison life was fairly monotonous, so I spent a lot of time reading. I'd let my imagination run away from me. I could lose hours.

Scott visited me in late September, bringing with him a birthday card from Mum, Dave and the girls. And another one from Ga, hers filled with a couple of scratchies. He'd lost the childhood softness of his face. And he'd cut his hair.

'Thanks for coming, Scott.'

'You know Mum hasn't even told the girls.'

'Fair enough, I suppose.'

'I told her to come with me but she had something on.'

'I'm glad you're here.'

'The Tigers are in the grand final. This afternoon.'

'Who are they playing?'

'South Fremantle.'

'Good chance then. Are you going?'

'Yeah.'

'We'll have it on the radio, I'm sure.'

I hugged him tight as he stood up to leave. A lump rose in my throat but I pushed it back down.

'Go the Tiges!' he shouted back over his shoulder as he walked out through the iron-barred doors.

As he was leaving, I remembered something I'd wanted to tell him. When he went to school – at Swanbourne – there were all these Scotts. Maybe five other Scotts in his class. Scott Stutridge, Scott Underwood, Scott Burrum. There was a run of Scotts!

'Remember that?' I was going to say. 'That there was a run of Scotts?'

One of the guards escorted me back to Main Division. This bloke wasn't too bad. I think he was one of Archie Butterly's guys actually. That's probably why he never gave me trouble.

Russell was in our cell, asleep. I switched on the wireless and tuned it to *Grandstand* in time for the game. There was still half an hour at least until bounce-down. The commentators, old Subi veterans, were crapping on about who was going to kick a bag – Rioli for Souths – and who was lacking form – Daniels for Claremont. The Krakouer brothers were bound to do something magic, they said. I thought I'd sneak a shit in before it started, lest I be disturbed at a crucial point in the game. The flush of the toilet must have woken up Russell, because shortly after he swung his big hairy legs over the bottom bunk and slapped his feet on the concrete floor.

'What's the time?' he asked, rubbing his eyes.

'Nearly one pm.'

'Fuck!' he said, standing up. 'I'm missing the races.' Russell snatched the wireless off the makeshift desk we'd made of crates and plywood and started furiously tuning it.

'Mate, I'm listening to the grand final.'

'I don't give a fuck. I've got money on the horses.' He didn't even look up from the wireless, just kept turning the wheel to find the right station, being met with alternating periods of silence and piercing white noise.

'It's my team playing.'

'I said I don't give a fuck!' He was looking up at me now. He'd found the station.

'Stay tuned for race three at Gloucester Park, due in less than two minutes,' announced the commentator.

'Mate, this isn't even the horses. It's the trots.'

'Shut the fuck up, cunt, or I'll knock you out. I swear to God,' he said, his fist ominously clenched.

I was shaking but I couldn't move. His eyes were black. I couldn't get out of my head the image that I'd seen in the newspaper of the young girl he raped and bashed.

'So?' he said, threatening.

I just shook my head and climbed up to my bunk and lay down on my side, staring at the wall. Tears rolled down my left cheek, disappearing into my pillow.

The way you could feel the outside temperature so acutely from inside the prison walls reminded me a lot of Marine Parade. I really wished I had the option of sleeping on the verandah though. When summer rolled around it was fucking hot. And everyone stank of body odour. Again, not too dissimilar to Marine Parade. But I felt a lot less comfortable calling these guys out on their hygiene than how I would with the boys back home.

I spent all of my free time studying English. There was always another bloody test. We'd have to sit down in a room and read some set reading, then write a whole essay on a question. It was fucking hard. But I kept reading and memorising quotes from books so I could parrot them back. I was lucky I had a good memory. Bud told me if I passed the Leaving Certificate then it'd look good for me when I was up for parole.

I really liked Old Jack. He had so many amazing stories about the Second World War. He reminded me of Pope in that he had a cheek about him. He could really have fun. And he was a natural storyteller. One of those people who brings the whole room along with them for the journey when they start telling a story. The kind of storyteller whose eyes glint at the climactic scenes and whose emphasis drops at the most opportune moments. But Old Jack also reminded me of

Jempa in a way. The war had definitely broken him too.

Every morning at seven am we stood out front of our open cells for roll call and inspection. One particular morning Old Jack had a glimmer in his eye. He started giggling and couldn't stop. And I tell you, it was infectious. Soon the whole division had lit up, bloke after bloke buckled over in laughter. The guards lost their shit. So they sent Old Jack to the kangaroo court. Sent a judge down and everything. Charged the old fella with 'laughing on parade'.

'How do you plead?' asked the judge of Old Jack.

'Not guilty, Your Honour. To the charge of laughing on parade anyway.'

The judge cocked his eyebrow at Old Jack. 'Not guilty?' he asked.

'Guilty to the lesser crime. Of smiling with intent.'

Apparently even the judge laughed then. But he still sent him to the chokey for two weeks for his sins.

The Tigers did win the premiership, after all. And I had the strangest thought. I wondered if my old man had gone to watch it. I knew he'd played for Claremont before I was born. One of the coaches at Swanny told this story once, of the old man playing for the Tigers and getting taken out, losing his contact lenses in the process. Everyone on the ground just about had to drop to their hands and knees to find them in the grass. The opposing team and all. I couldn't remember the last time I thought about him. Years maybe.

I finished my High School Leaving English Certificate. I was in the top twenty per cent. That was a shock. I was just happy to pass. I celebrated by playing Bud in a round of Test match cricket, explaining to him the rules of the game as we set up our little cardboard sides. The batting and the fielding. The overs. The innings. The great West Australian Test cricketers – Kim Hughes, Dennis Lillee and Rod Marsh. Bud spun the wheel. Full toss. He hit a six.

'So it's like baseball?'

'I suppose it is a bit. But you just run between the two bases until you're out.'

'And it goes for five days.' I could tell Bud was sceptical from his tone.

I smiled. 'Sometimes it only takes four.'

Bud talked to me about the union. He was in the school-teacher's union, he said. That right-wing leaders around the world like Thatcher and Reagan were threatening fairness in the workplace. And that it was important to protect those rights here. That there was power in collectivism.

'Why do you think they keep you blokes here separate?' he asked.

I shook my head.

'Because if you got together, you'd overpower them, easy. They're shit-scared of you working together. So they keep you apart.'

I was back at Lyall Street. Up a tree. Looking down at the house. If I strained my eyes, I could see Ga through the window in the kitchen, behind the sink. She couldn't see me. I couldn't see the rest of them. Pippin and Scott. And Jempa. Where were they? I climbed higher and higher up the Moreton Bay fig, craning my neck to look into the backyard. The door of the outhouse was wide open. The door into the shed was unlocked but closed.

Russell's snoring woke me up. It wasn't that loud, but he'd rolled over and it exploded out of him in a sharp snort and it startled me. So I sat up on the top bunk and looked out the window into the dark, listening to the wireless. ABC Radio 2. They were saying something about how the government was winding back Medibank. Whitlam's fund for free healthcare. I didn't think that was right. So I listened to caller after caller admonish the government for such a thing. *Things haven't been right in this godforsaken country since the Dismissal!* someone said. Russell turned over in his sleep. Another host was droning on now, one of the late-night hosts they'd put on with low, radio-worthy voices with near-British accents.

Then a tinkle of piano keys.

Then horns, trumpets, trombone.

Then saxophone.

The voice crooned out of the wireless. I couldn't hear anything else. Nothing. Not even Russell's breath right below me.

'Georgia on My Mind'.

I thought of Ga. I thought of what pain she must have endured. Suffering from diphtheria in early childhood. Witnessing the zeppelins over Walker-on-Tyne – a coal-mining town by the Scottish border – in 1914 and hiding in the bathroom on her hands and knees while sirens flooded her ears. Sailing to the other side of the world for a chance at a better life, leaving behind everyone she knew. Falling in love and then losing her husband to the next war – back three years later but never the same. Alone. Grappling with the polio outbreak of the forties, which reached two of her own children in Perth – disabling them for life.

Horns, trumpets, trombone.

She raised her children, only to then take her grandchildren on. Trying to keep them safe and secure at the same time her husband took to drink and violence to heal his wounds. And who mostly took his hatred of war and of the world out on the innocent.

I thought about the fact that I wouldn't be alive if it weren't for her. And I wondered whether I wanted to be alive at all. I don't know if I'd thought that consciously before. I felt like I'd been trying to work out that very question my whole life.

The horns built up into a crescendo in a perfect marriage with the drums.

Then silence.

***

Bud organised a transfer for me to Pardelup Prison Farm where he worked, around the same time I found out that Peter had been busted and was en route to Freo. A reward for good behaviour, as well as the high score on the English Leaving Certificate, I supposed. They sat me down with the psychiatrist and the doctor and the judge and they gave me the all clear. I was sad to leave Old Jack. He was still in the chokey when I left. The farm was better than Freo. I could breathe there. We'd play basketball and cricket and work on the land. Bud even helped us build cricket nets. The Noongar blokes on the farm taught us their dream stories. They explained how the European seasons were out of place here in the South West. That there's actually six seasons on Noongar country.

Bud organised excursions for us too, to rivers and places by the ocean, like Greens Pool in Denmark. We'd go swimming and catch abalone off the rocks and bring them back and cook them. I loved being on country. The Noongar blokes, however, treated the Great Southern land with awe and suspicion. Apparently, a war had been fought there between the mobs, and a lot of people died.

Pardelup didn't feel like prison. Much less of a prison than Rotto or being a junky had been. Less of a prison than either side of Stirling Highway for that matter. I felt free to be simply alone with the land.

One day Bud came by my room at the farm, and I could tell by the look on his face that he had news.

'So your parole meeting has been scheduled for next week,' Bud said. He was sitting on the edge of my bed. I'd been imprisoned for about fifteen months now, one month shy of my minimum sentence. It had somehow simultaneously taken forever to get to that point and, at the same time, no time at all.

'Yeah, I know.'

'They're not going to let you out if you don't have a home to go to.'

I realised I couldn't go back home. I mean, I had to, obviously. But Bud and a couple of other guys and I had watched *The Man with the Golden Arm* – some Sinatra movie – and in it he realises that he'll never get off the gear if he doesn't get out of the scene. And I'm not sure if that was really the point of the story at all, but it made sense to me. I needed fresh air.

I didn't say anything to Bud. I just looked up to meet his eyes. He had a sad smile on his face like he felt real sorry for me. I didn't know what to say, so I just nodded. He got up, squeezed my shoulder and left the room. I walked out into the common room to the phone booth and decided to call Mum.

PART THREE

1983–1988

THE MERMAID AND THE GULLY MONSTER

When Peter got out of prison too, we drove up north in his Valiant. He'd been done for possession or something. Before he went inside, he'd been working up in Dampier, and he told me the money and footy was good. I'd decided I needed to get out of Perth. So it was about March 1983 when we finally hit the road. We drove for hours through barren red land. Little specks of green swallowed by brown. The rivers looked like arteries and veins. The dry lakes cracked lips and furrowed brows. The dark of the water like blood and moisture pooling in the crook of an elbow.

Peter was tailgating the car in front of us. A cream Ford Laser. Probably an old duck, I thought.

'Creepin' Jesus,' I said.

We were in a single lane. Straight enough to overtake but the opposite lane was heavy with trucks. It wouldn't have been advisable to risk it. We awaited the reprieve of an overtaking lane. But when it came, the old duck put her foot down.

'Why do they always speed up in the overtaking lane? Christ.'

I couldn't help but laugh. Peter slammed his foot down and sped past her in the left lane. We both turned our heads to the right just as he drew level with her, either to shoot her an incensed look or otherwise see how stupid she looked and whether it matched the image her driving was projecting to the world. It was a young bloke. In hi-vis. Punching a dart.

'You can never pick 'em,' said Peter.

'Stupidity knows no bounds.'

We stopped in Geraldton for petrol and sausage rolls. My old man lived there, I knew that. Pippin had told me. I wondered vaguely what I'd say to him if I saw him there, at the servo. The thought made me nervous.

'Ready?' asked Peter, scrunching up his paper bag and chucking it in the bin next to me, sweeping the pastry off his shirt.

'Let's get out of here.'

We passed burnt-out cars. Dark-red dirt and termite mounds and spinifex. Trees that grew against all odds and trees with trunks as white as bone. Wild cows and bush tomatoes. Vast nothing. We drove for hours without seeing another servo. I felt an urge to ask Peter to pull over and walk out into the bush just to see what was out there. But I knew we'd never make it back. The sky was bluer than in the city, set against the red dirt. I felt insignificant.

Peter mucked around with the radio, tuning it until he found a station that worked.

'–after declaring victory at the weekend, former ACTU National President Bob Hawke has been sworn in as Australia's twenty-third prime minister, the convincing win cementing his mandate for promised industrial relations reform and reconciliation. He is in Canberra and will announce his cabinet in the coming days.'

Peter and I looked at each other. I smiled.

'Long live the king.'

When we reached the town, the Jesus statue welcomed us with wide-open arms.

***

The traditional owners will tell you that Dampier is where everything began. Throughout history, Indigenous mobs migrated there from all over the country. Their connection to the land in Dampier is so strong that when they die, wherever they are, their souls return there. Five different Aboriginal language groups call the archipelago home: the Ngarluma, Yaburara, Mardudhunera, Yindjibarndi and the Wong-Goo-Tt-Oo. The endless mountains of red rocks that look like they've been excavated in a mining operation are actually tens of thousands of years old.

We walked down to Barnacle Bob's for fish and chips. And dim sims. When we reached the peninsula, the sun had just set over the ocean. The lights of the port and North West Shelf infrastructure on the Burrup looked like a city floating on water. You could see the masts of the boats sunk by a cyclone poking their heads out of the drink.

We found home at the Mermaid Hotel, where a bloke called Bondy was holding court at the front bar and German backpackers were serving up beers. Bondy was tall, well built, with a huge ginger beard. He sported the northerner uniform of singlet and stubbies, with a stubby in hand. He could have been the bloke on the Export can.

The Mermaid shared a car park with the cop shop, and the coppers were usually somewhere in between. The beer garden outside had no garden and was just a gable roof with fans whirring underneath and a stage where a band was setting up. Inside, the air-con was cranked up so high it was freezing. Ace was in his corner sipping vodka on the rocks, his hair slicked back, tattoos dark against his white skin.

There were a couple of dogs under his feet. There were pool tables in between dining tables pushed up against TVs, and a TAB squeezed into the corner. Everyone was smoking.

A couple of the boys from the Dampier Sharks were there having warm-up beers before footy training.

'You've got your boots in the car, right? Come down with us,' said Bondy.

I'd already had a couple of pints at that point so I was unsure about my training capacity, but Bondy reassured me. 'Mate, I've been here since three pm.'

So Peter and I rolled down to Windy Ridge. It was after dark but it was still hot. A few of the boys were kicking the footy around. Ducky – the head coach – came down from the club with a bag of shirts and a stack of cones. We jogged a lap and talked some shit. It felt good to have a footy back in my hands. We split off with the rezzies and ran drills for a bit. Jacko was a killer, a natural athlete. He was a classic Victorian midfielder. He had a footy mullet and kind brown eyes. Fish and Clarky, both locals, played in the goals. Fish was a goal sneak and Clarky was a show pony. Bullant was around the middle. He was fucking crazy. Similar to the unpredictable units I'd met in prison. Great bloke, but trouble. The Train, built like a brick shithouse, played fullback. Ducky picked me for a ruckman because of my height. I hadn't really played in the ruck before. There was no colts team that year, so Bondy's son – Young Bondy – was out having a kick with us. He was pretty solid for fourteen. Looked a lot like his old man.

I tired pretty quickly. My lungs and chest ached. Peter, however, was pushing for A grade. He must have spent his time inside at the gym instead of dealing cigarettes. There was a couple of weeks until the season started proper, but Ducky told us we'd have a scratchy against the Karratha Kats that Saturday.

'We have to get Sammy up here,' I said to Peter.

We trudged back home to the Mermaid. The band was playing now. I pulled up next to Bondy at the front bar and sank a few pints. Not enough to get too silly, but enough that I lost count.

'Red Dog was a stinky old thing. We were kicking him out of the pub all the time,' some old bloke said.

'You missed the cyclone last year. Biggest in years, I reckon. The eye went right over us,' another old bloke said.

Bondy warned us about the gully monster.

'Watch out tonight if you're heading back to the units over there. If you've had a couple,' he flicked my pint glass with his middle finger, 'that's when it gets you.'

'I have to go around it. Been done too many times. Takes an extra fifteen minutes for me to get home,' said Webby's mum, Deb.

Bondy also warned us about Marg. 'She rules this place with an iron fist, I tell you. If she says last drinks, she means last drinks.'

Bondy introduced me to Terry, who worked at Hamersley Iron. Terry reminded me a bit of old Andrew from TAFE. He seemed smart and kind.

'Grant here is looking for work at HI,' Bondy said.

'Got a trade?' Terry asked.

'Nope.'

'How about you come on as my assistant then?'

'Yeah, sure.'

'Electrical,' added Terry.

'Great,' I said. Not really knowing the difference either way.

Webby was in the band that was playing out the back, Mr Meaner. I knew Webby from back in Perth. He kicked around with a few of the Swanny boys. I think he knew Scott. He was a quiet sort of bloke.

'Are you still playing, mate?' he asked.

'Guitar – yeah.'

'That's great. There's a strong music scene up here. Could use another guitarist in this jazz outfit I'm gigging with, if you're interested.'

'Sounds like you need a new guitarist in this outfit too.'

Webby laughed. 'It was a bit average tonight, wasn't it.'

'You could say that.'

'I'll keep you in mind.'

I got to talking to Jacko and we made plans to surf the next day. He'd been up north for about six months now. He liked chess too. And cricket.

'How about that seventy-three series in the Caribbean? Forty-four beers or something they knocked off on the flight. Marsh and Walters, was it?' I asked.

'How about when Dougie Walters was up all night on the piss, trying to get Kerry to come out, and he wouldn't, and he cracked the shits at them. So Dougie and Marsh got absolutely pisswrecked, and Kerry the next morning was all obnoxious and calling them clowns and everything. And then he got out after one run on a block!' said Jacko.

'Yeah, and then Dougie gave him shit right out there in the middle of the pitch.'

'Yeah, he said to him as he was walking off, "So are you coming out on the piss tonight?"'

Jacko cracked up. His laugh was infectious.

'What's the go with the gully monster?' I asked.

'Well, every gully has a different monster,' he said. 'The one out here is particularly vicious. Combination of how heavy the piss is and how steep the gully is, I reckon.'

At around eleven that night, Marg called last drinks so we ordered a few and downed them quick. I stumbled outside and lit up a cigarette. It was still pretty hot. I clocked a phone booth across the car park by the bottle-o and I walked over to it and rang Sam.

'Hello?'

'Hey mate, it's Grant.'

'Hey mate.'

'Look, you should get up here to the Pilbara. Play footy.'

'I'm meant to be playing for South Fremantle this year.'

'Just think about it. You'd love it.'

'The surf?'

'Checking it out tomorrow. Apparently it bloody pumps before a cyclone.'

'Yeah, okay.'

The telephone clicked off and went silent. I didn't have any coins to call again. I wandered back across the car park to the verandah out the front of the Mermaid, and Peter and I made plans to leave, mapping a route in our heads. Wary of the gully monster.

THE NULLARBOR

They gathered their things quick. There had been a suffocating feeling in the house since the robbery. Even though they barred the windows shut and the door was deadlocked. The cash leftover from their MG trade-in weighed heavy in Susie's suitcase. It was like they were missing one of the foundation blocks of Maslow's hierarchy of needs – security. They weren't safe. And so everything they did was only about survival. It was impossible to feel content. Before they even got on Great Eastern Highway Susie remembered she'd left her curling iron on in the bathroom, but she didn't bother saying anything. They stopped for petrol in Ascot. Charlie filled up and Susie went inside the roadhouse to order a bucket of hot chips. Charlie came in, paid, and then walked about out again, while Susie waited. It took at least fifteen minutes. Susie felt that sick, squirming feeling in her stomach while she waited. By the time they were ready she wasn't even hungry anymore.

The Land Cruiser was nearly moving when she climbed back in. Charlie pulled back violently onto Great Eastern Highway, barely checking the lane. His hands were white on the steering wheel. Susie was too scared to move, she just held the bucket of chips and felt them go cold between her hands. It was hard to tell how long it had been any because Charlie had the radio turned down. But the chips were stone cold. There started to be a distance between each town of Perth's eastern fringes, with a lot of empty space in between. Susie was thinking electric thoughts and was struggling to keep up with them. Soon enough she was in another place and she realised she was dreaming.

Once they drove past Southern Cross and the sun was in the rear-view and the little green sign on the left indicated 225 kilometres until Kalgoorlie, Charlie felt his jaw unclench. He didn't say anything, just placed his left hand on Susie's knee and rubbed it a little. He felt her leg inch up, leaning into him. He probably should have left out the key for his aunty, he thought. He imagined his mum's face upon realising he was gone again and felt his shoulders tense up. Then he shook it off. They needed to get out of Perth. If they never went back, he'd be happy.

Susie was busting to piss so bad that she couldn't wait

until they got into town, so they pulled into the petrol station at Coolgardie. Charlie rolled down the window and lit up a cigarette while he waited. The air felt different here than in Perth. He felt lighter. He savoured every drag of his smoke, inhaling deep, occasionally tapping it over the lip of the ashtray. When Susie jumped back in, he kissed her on the cheek. She smiled. He started up the engine and she picked up the bucket of chips from the console and had a couple cold.

It was getting dark when they got to the motel. Charlie swore under his breath at the price of it, picking singles from the bundle of pineapples between an elastic band he pulled from his pocket. The place must double as a brothel, Charlie thought, judging by the clientele. The room was small but clean. Susie jumped into the shower and Charlie sat down on the twin bed, rubbing his hands over the same scratchy green blanket he'd seen at his mum's place, and leaned his head against the pine-coloured, wood-panelled wall.

He really felt like a fix but all their smack had been stolen back at Cottesloe. And Susie was off it anyway. He probably could've gone back to the lobby and spoken to one of the girls there – they'd know where to pick up some dope. But he couldn't move. He was tired. The only thing he could focus on was the sound of the water running in the shower, and the loud slaps of it against Susie's body reverberating through the bathroom.

In the morning they smoked a joint and drank black coffees on the plastic chairs by the front door of their room that faced into the car park. Then they drove south. It must have been hours but it felt like no time at all that they reached the border. Charlie felt relaxed. Susie was hiding behind her huge black sunnies. Charlie slowed the Land Cruiser, entering the queue. There was only a handful of cars in front. He could feel the stash of pot in the flap of the door jutting against his knee. When they reached the front the man in the turret just silently nodded his head and lifted the boom gate. Charlie looked over at Susie, whose jaw had dropped, and laughed.

'Well, that's gotta be our smoothest drug run over the border yet, hasn't it?' said Charlie.

Susie imagined herself in a little boat in the ocean, looking up at the enormity of the cliffs. They consumed her. It made her feel sad. The Eyre Highway hugged the coastline as they drove east along the Great Australian Bight. The cliffs, orange against a deep blue, were sharp, violent. Ancient.

Gravel crunched under the wheels of the Land Cruiser as Charlie pulled into a shoulder at Fowlers Bay. They got out and took a track of hard, stony, white sand up to a lookout. Charlie held Susie's hand tight. When they got to the top, Susie crouched on the ground and rolled a joint. Charlie hovered his arms around her, shielding her from the wind. Susie sparked up and stood up, leaning against Charlie who leaned against the distressed, wooden frame of the barrier. The ocean was indistinguishable from the sky. Charlie imagined whales beneath the surface – old creatures who lurked for decades and rarely bothered to come up for air. He thought about what the Dutch or the Chinese or whoever came first felt when they saw it – where they now were. Charlie felt his feet in his shoes dig into the rocky sand, anchored to the ground. It felt unreal.

They went back to the Land Cruiser when it started to get cold. Maybe they'd stay the night in Penong, or drive straight through to Ceduna. Maybe not. Charlie suppressed a yawn in his throat. He pulled back onto the highway and Susie started rolling another joint.

Charlie thought he'd never love anyone like he did Susie.

DAMPIER SINGLE QUARTERS

Hamersley Iron set me up in a self-contained unit at the single quarters. It had a shower and a toilet and was stumbling distance from Windy Ridge. It was perfect. My unit was among maybe ten others, set out in a rectangle around a grassed area with a barbecue and picnic set-up in the middle. Almost every night there'd be people out there having beers and jamming. We started a band called Bits and Pieces, made up of all different cultures and ethnicities, with me the only white guy in the troupe. People from all over the world had moved up north for the mining boom. So the single quarters was something of a cosmopolitan hub. There was always someone cooking something incredible, a hāngī or smoked meats on the Weber. And there was always beer. It was truly a multicultural melting pot.

I started out as an electrician's assistant to Terry in the workshop. Our uniform was workboots, a pair of stubbies and a t-shirt. Which was a blessing in the blistering heat, but a curse when I was forced to hold the bottom of the ladder for Terry, who almost never wore undies and frequently dropped a nutsack through his stubbies. It was easy work, if a little boring.

A couple of months in, I moved onto the port – operating. There was more money in it, being shiftwork. I operated the stackers and the reclaimers, all by hand. That's all probably done by computer these days, in some room in the Perth CBD. But back then I was at Parker Point, operating the shiploader. The first time on shift, the foreman showed me up to the little cabin on the boom, right on the end. It felt precarious. A tugboat went past on a big wave and it moved the ship in front of me. The big bridge of the ship floated higher and higher over the peak of the wave, flooding my vision, closing the gap between the cabin and the side of the ship. My stomach dropped. I felt like I was on a ferris wheel. I grabbed the rail hard and braced myself. The foreman cracked up.

'That's just a trick of the eyes. Feels like you're moving,' the foreman said. 'You'll get used to it.'

Operating the shiploader was a logistical nightmare. The shiploader itself was a cabin on rails which went up and down with a big boom arm that swung left to right. Basically, I filled the export ships with iron ore. But each ship was different: it had different masts to navigate the boom arm around and different hatch sizes and quantities to deploy to get the ore in. And it wasn't as simple as moving mechanically from one hatch to the next, because if you overfilled one side of the ship it would stress the hull, and the whole ship would begin to tilt. Kind of like if you put the washing all on one side of the clothes horse without balancing it as you go, then you're in trouble. You had to fill it up in little batches spread evenly across the available hatches. So when you moved the boom arm to the next hatch you'd need the guy operating the system to hold the ore until you were safely over an open hatch. It was dicey. We were the last point of production before export, handling the most expensive and precious grade of ore. You'd be in the shit if you lost any of it.

One time I was on night shift when I started nodding off in my chair. I'd played footy that day and was exhausted, but I got no sleep in the arvo because it was too hot and the boys around the barbecue were making too much noise. Anyway, I'd nodded off in my chair and I woke up to a Japanese sailor screaming. The ship was tilted on one side. I shat myself and quickly moved to load the other side but the hatch door wasn't fully open yet, and by the time I navigated the huge mast of the ship it was too late. Approximately twenty tonnes of iron ore missed the ship and hit the deck – 'deck cargo', we called it. The other blokes came off their machines groaning with their shovels and helped me get it down the hatch. I decided I'd avoid the sneers at the wet mess that night.

Dampier was so good for me. It probably sounds crazy, but I felt the warm air thawing my body and my soul from the inside out. It was the fresh air that I'd wanted.

I'd been gigging around with Webby's cabaret band, New Profile. We played the Roving Jockey Club, the Red Cross ball. Formal sorts of events with dancing. Webby's mum, Deb, played sax with us, with a few other locals on guitar, bass and drums. Cabaret passed the time. But Webby and I were more interested in rock-and-roll.

I missed my family. And the old boys. Pippin was in Kalgoorlie at that time. And Scott was still at home, or he'd just moved out. I was desperate for an anchor between my old life and now, so I could be certain my new life was real.

Sam moved up north in 1984. And the next day we went for a surf. The swell wasn't as good as it gets before a cyclone, but it was big enough.

'Where's the best break?' asked Sam.

The best break was the southern tip of Sam's Island.

'Sam's Island?'

'Not you, mate. Old Sam. Sam Ostojich.'

Old Sam was an immigrant from Yugoslavia who built himself a home on the island in 1966 out of rocks and organic materials. There was no electricity or running water. He just lived there, off the land. It was a fair paddle out to the island but that didn't perturb Sam. There were waves. Right hands. It felt good to have Sam up there.

Afterwards Old Sam had coffees waiting for us, and he showed us around his home he'd built with his bare hands. He had a bit of a stoop from an injury from the railways which had permanently incapacitated him decades earlier. He moved around alright, though. He'd planted palm trees and built a stone wall around his house and the outdoor area structure. Decorated with coral and shells.

Webby eventually sacked the other guitarist in Mr Meaner and got me in, as well as a couple of the other blokes from HI. We were playing at the Mermaid in Dampier and the Walkabout Hotel in Karratha just about every weekend. Just covers, basically. But it was going off.

I started to build up a tan from the red dirt that soaked into my skin. Cyclone season was over. The days started to get cooler, but they were mostly an easy thirty degrees at least. I certainly didn't miss Perth winter. Plus I didn't even notice the flies anymore.

I signed up to be the shop steward at work. Our union was The Australian Workers' Union. You could always tell when a strike was on by the number of boats in the car park. So when Tommy – one of the sparkies onsite – asked me along to my first stop-work meeting and there were no boats out the front, I was sorely disappointed. Tommy was a hoot. Larger than life. Dan was the AWU organiser for the Pilbara. He played the saxophone and sported a killer moustache. Dan was chairing the meeting.

'Look, now we've done the formalities, I think Johnny had an urgent issue from Robe River. John?'

'Yeah, principally about safety. They're cutting corners all over the shop. The reclaimers are being overfilled, like way too heavy to be safe. But instead of smaller loads, they're just chucking counterweights on the other side of the thing, to weigh it down!'

'Get fucked,' said Harv. Harv was a delegate. But he looked more like a bikie than a union guy.

'No joke. I've tried bringing it up with the foreman, but he's giving me peanuts.'

'I'll speak to state office about organising an inspection,' said Harv.

'Like, those machines are not designed to take that weight,' said Dan.

All the blokes nodded.

'It's bullshit. Someone's going to die out there,' said John.

I also enjoyed the union meetings because it gave me a chance to speak. There were practical issues to solve, helping others. Organising boycotts and solidarity protests. I had agency for the first time in my life. There was a buzz among the old unionists because of Hawkie. A prime minister who spoke for us, we thought. Hope. There was already talk of a second Accord. Our pay rises had started to hit our bank accounts, at least. I started saving money for the first time in my life.

That year we played Wickham in the grand final. I was in the goals. Sam was on the wing.

One of the guys on Wickham's bench was giving Sam the shits. Near quarter time I ran for some water, and while I was chatting to the runner, we heard him from the dugout.

'Fuck you, black cunt.'

Sam took a hanger right in front of the guy and kicked a goal to level the score. But I could see by his face it was getting to him.

We lost our legs in the second quarter. At half-time, Ducky gave us a spray. I grabbed a water and a slice of orange out of the esky. It was ice-cold. With more beers than waters.

'Only a Nor'-westerner knows how to pack an esky,' said Bullant.

In the third, Sam was on the wing near the arsehole on the bench. When he lined up for goal, the guy went feral at him. Halfway through the quarter, when Sam hit the post, I could hear the prick laughing and jeering from where I was loitering in the backline. Ducky moved me back up front. When I passed Sam, I tapped his elbow.

'Don't worry about that prick.'

'I'm not worried,' said Sam.

Someone kicked a goal down the other end. The umpire's whistle sounded. Wickham swapped their subs in while the play had stopped. The prick finally ran out onto the field. His tail up, buoyed by the six-goal deficit we were looking at. He ran straight to Sam with a fat smile on his face. Before he could get word out, Sam wound his arm back and swung his fist into the bloke's face. A king hit. If you didn't see it, you'd have heard it. The crack. The prick flew through the air and landed flat on his back. He was knocked out. The runners carted him off. The umpires sounded the whistle to resume play. The prick didn't play a single minute of the game. Wickham were fuming.

They killed us in the end, by nine goals or something. But the mood at the Mermaid was electric. Everyone was talking about Sam.

'The look on that cunt's face as you clocked him!' said Bullant.

'After he'd been waiting to run out all game.'

'Will he even get a premiership medal? He didn't technically play!'

Sam just smiled, shaking his head. He was our best on ground.

Then it was cyclone season again. At work we reinforced ship lines daily, making sure everything was tied down or else double-bolted to the ground. But nothing happened. It rained once or twice. That was about it.

I was playing with Mr Meaner at the Walkabout when I first met Di. It was a Friday night. We were playing there every second Friday at that stage. They let us keep our gear there all packed in the corner so we didn't have to lug it around. She was there with Webby's sister. They worked together at Woodside. Webby introduced us in the break. She told me later that she'd already decided by then, when she first saw me on stage.

Di was beautiful. She was tall with dark brown hair and pale blue eyes. Her parents worked on the Commonwealth Railways so she grew up alongside train stations and workshops, from Port Augusta to Kalgoorlie. She had a country Australian twang in her voice. She was down-to-earth. She had a truck driver's licence. She was funny. When I met her, she was living with her mum after her dad died, before moving up north to spend time with her brother. She worked as a security guard at the Burrup. She'd had a failed marriage already, so she wasn't going to put up with any bullshit. That scared me and kind of comforted me at the same time. She made me feel safe. We got together. I stayed with her in Millars Well in Karratha, near the pub, for days that became weeks and then when I left, she came with me to the single quarters, and we started saving for a house.

It was in the workshop in 1986 where I first saw the front page of the *West Australian*, saying that Charlie had been arrested in Malaysia for drug trafficking and was facing the death penalty. I'd heard Susie had died in a car accident somewhere East maybe six months before.

It didn't feel real. I felt guilty. When I'd been busted, I didn't for a second think about mentioning Charlie. But maybe I should have. I probably could have checked in on him after hearing about Susie too. I'd moved on with my own life, so it felt like everyone else had too.

BERKELEY CRESCENT

Di and I bought a four-by-two on Berkeley Crescent. Well, bought inasmuch as was possible in Dampier at the time when HI owned everything in town. It was a brown-brick house with big windows, a bright pink bougainvillea tree in the front yard and a corrugated-iron roof strapped down for cyclones. Our grass was green despite the heat, as was everyone else's in the street, because HI subsidised the water.

It felt like I'd known Di my whole life. We just fit. She made me feel home. At times I imagined that I'd forgotten my life before her.

It was July 1986. We were watching GWN News. The lead story was that Charlie had been hanged in Malaysia. I felt the blood rush to my face. The other guy who got caught, the young kid, had been killed too. They showed footage of Charlie walking into the courtroom. Photos of the young kid with his family. I thought about Charlie and Susie. I thought about being interrogated by the detective and Dick at the lock-up after I got caught. Maybe if I'd ratted on Charlie, then I would have saved his life.

I thought about telling Di all of this.

I got up and got another beer.

The foreman was on leave, so Harv was acting foreman. Harv was our leading hand and one of the AWU shop stewards. A big, hard union bloke with tattoos and his shirt sleeves ripped off. And Tommy was enjoying having a crack at his new-found authority.

'Just shut the fuck up, Tommy, and get on with it,' Harv said.

'Mate, you've got a bad attitude,' said Tommy.

'Don't push me.'

'I'm calling a stop-work meeting to discuss this. Come on, boys,' said Tommy, waving his arms in a sweeping motion towards the exit door. So we downed tools. Harv, being a union member himself, came along too. We stood outside, smoking, while Tommy chaired the meeting.

'Our foreman today has a bad attitude, wouldn't you all agree?'

The circle of union members nodded. Harv shook his head.

'I say we strike,' said Tommy.

The boys' cheers drowned out Harv's protestations. And then we walked out. To the Mermaid. Harv grudgingly in tow. He had a good time explaining it to his wife, who happened to be at the pub that very lunchtime.

'So you walked off because the foreman had a bad attitude.'

'Yep.'

'But you're the foreman.'

'Yep.'

'So you walked off… in protest of… yourself?' Harv's missus was not happy.

'Well, I'm not a scab.'

The boys cheered again.

'Shouldn't you boys be at the wet mess?' asked Marg, pouring out another round of pints.

'We're on strike, Marg. Technically that'd be crossing the picket.'

'Plus Tommy's barred,' I said.

'I'm not barred!' said Tommy. 'I barred myself.'

'Why's that, love?' asked Marg.

'Well, a couple of weeks ago I got pissed and left the Valiant there. Then the next day I went to pick it up but got pissed again and had to leave the EH. Then the next day I left my bike. Then Harv dropped me off, but I got pissed again.

And then on the sixth day the missus came in her Datsun 120Y to pick me up and got pissed too!'

Everyone laughed.

'So it's just no good for me, you see.'

'Well, you're safe here,' said Marg.

An old bloke was in the TAB corner of the pub, holding a fistful of tickets, staring up at the TV.

'Run third, ya prick!' he yelled.

A few pints down and I was getting philosophical with Tommy.

'Glad you're up here, mate. Enjoying it?' Tommy asked.

'I love it.'

'And the work?'

'It's alright,' I said, smiling down at my beer. 'I don't know how long I want to be working with my body, though.'

'You're no orphan,' said Tommy, unconsciously running his hand over his injured knee.

'But yeah, the money's good. I can't complain.'

'Have you thought about doing your apprenticeship?'

'Yeah, a couple of the blokes have told me to look into it. I'm probably a bit old, though.'

'Will be worth it in the long run, but.'

'Yeah, but I just bought a house.'

Tommy nodded into his beer.

The bougainvillea was a shocking pink, almost purple now. The bees seemed to love it. Petals would float to the ground and sit on the driveway with bees buzzing around them until the piles got large enough for me to sweep them up and deposit them back in the garden.

Mr Meaner was getting big. We played the Walkabout or the Mermaid every weekend. And when bigger acts came to town, they had us on first. We supported Mental as Anything and Ian Moss. And then we supported GANGgajang, in front of thousands. Women in the crowd would be up on people's shoulders pulling up their tops to show us their tits. It was truly something else.

One afternoon at the wet mess I got to talking to some of the electricians. Ever since working as Terry's assistant I'd been interested, I suppose. It seemed like the sparkies worked more with their heads than their hands.

'They've just opened the applications for next year's apprenticeships. Why don't you apply?' asked one of the sparkies.

'Yeah, you should go for it!' said another.

'You might get to work with me again,' said Terry, with a wink.

I shuddered at the thought of another minute spent staring at that man's nutsack through his stubbies.

'Yeah, I'll look into it,' I said.

When I got home, I could hear Di's screams from the driveway. I flung the front door open and ran inside. She was in the bathroom, her voice bouncing off the tiles.

'What's wrong?'

'There's a snake in the toilet!'

'Flush it down, for Christ's sake.'

'I'm not going near there!'

She was standing in the bath, brandishing the shit-brush like a weapon.

I tiptoed to the toilet. Sure enough, there was a snake in there – a brown snake. His little head poking up through the hole. A poo dragon. I held the big flush button down until he disappeared.

'He's gone now,' I said, looking up at her.

She stared back, stony-faced. 'I'm going to piss on the lawn.'

***

The months started to pass quick, like days. It was cooler at night but the water was always warm. I tried calling Scott around then, but I couldn't seem to catch him.

The Dampier Sharks rezzies made the finals. We were to play the Port Hedland Rovers on the Saturday. Having attended

Clarky's twenty-first the night before, I, for one, was dusty. I nearly spewed from sheer dread when I rocked up to the car park at Windy Ridge and saw the parked bus. Slim, the not-so-slim bus driver, was standing out the front ticking names off a sheet. I was shocked at how many of the boys were already on the bus. Fish had his head in a bucket. Bullant had a half-empty blue sports drink in his hand, sweat dripping down his forehead. Jacko and Peter were both a similar shade of grey. Sam clambered on the bus next, not actually looking half bad. He smiled at me as he sat down.

'You're younger, you can back it up,' I said. 'Wait until you get to my age.'

'Whatever, old man.'

We sat there for about ten minutes before Slim clambered into the driver's seat and set off. Clarky didn't make it. Ducky wasn't happy. No one spoke, except for pit-stop requests for a piss or a spew.

I kicked six goals in the first half. At half-time we were only two kicks behind. Ducky didn't even really give us a spray. He seemed to be genuinely impressed at how we'd pulled up. But then in the second half we ran out of steam. I lost my legs. I was struggling to breathe. Bullant spewed. Fish wanted to come out but we didn't have any subs. It was horrific. We ended up getting flogged. I stopped counting after seven. Ducky was ropable.

Back at Windy Ridge, Wayne – the footy club president – was leaning against the bar, waiting. He was one of those old blokes whose face was always flushed. Real beetroot-like, old Wayne.

He waited for most of the blokes to get through the door before he went off.

'You fucking rats!' he screamed, little bits of spit flying out of his mouth. 'You couldn't have waited until tonight to get ratshit?'

'It was a special occasion, sir,' said Bullant. I bit my lip to suppress a laugh.

'Special occasion? Pig's arse!'

Fish sniggered.

'And now you come here to drink my piss?'

'If you wouldn't mind?' said Bullant.

The boys buckled over. I had tears running down my face. Wayne's face had gone a deep shade of red.

'Goddamn rats!' he screamed, slamming his middy down on the bar and storming into the kitchen.

'Few pints of Swan, please, Pam,' said Fish.

Pam poured us a round.

'To the Dampier Rat Pack,' said Sam, charging his glass.

Around late 1987, the human resources manager at HI sent me application forms for an electrical apprenticeship.

Because I'd never finished high school, they needed me to do a maths test. It was a written exam. As soon as I opened the exam booklet, I knew I'd fail. I didn't recognise anything. I hadn't even prepared a cheat sheet like I used to for the exams back in my mechanical apprenticeship. I walked out after the mandatory half hour and went straight home.

'So what now?' asked Di, pouring me a red.

'They reckon they can put me in night school for the maths. Then apply again.'

'Where's that?'

'Karratha Technical College. It's a bridging course.'

'Well, why not?'

'I won't be able to do night shift anymore.'

'Well, for how long?'

'Just a year. But then if I get in it'll be another few.'

'Well, how about we see if you can get in first.'

'I won't be earning as much without shiftwork.'

'We'll work it out,' she said, smiling.

It might have been the red wine but it felt like we would.

So then I was attending night classes at the technical college and working the shiploader full-time. In the winter from the cabin I could see whales out over the peninsula, breaching on their route migrating north. I was still playing with Mr Meaner on weekends too, so I barely found time for the pub.

The next time I walked into the maths exam, I was quietly confident. As I flicked through the booklet in the preliminary reading time, the formulas and algorithms were no longer foreign. I didn't walk out feeling like I'd smashed it or anything, but I'd definitely passed. And exactly two weeks later, HI sent me an offer of placement for an electrical apprenticeship.

I often thought of Scott and Pippin. And Lyall Street. I was always speaking with Ga on the phone. Jempa had died. I think I was in a footy game or something, and someone ran afield to tell me. I don't think I even went to the funeral. I didn't speak to my siblings about it. Or Mum. We all just let it pass. Sometimes I'd think of Charlie and feel guilty all over again. I'd think of the thumping and whooshing sounds I'd imagined years earlier, echoing from the gallows at Fremantle. And then sometimes I wouldn't.

***

One late afternoon, Zeus was in the kitchen, sitting at Di's feet as she stirred whatever was cooking on the stove. Zeus was a gorgeous bluey-cross mutt thing. He wasn't our dog – he was Nigel's from across the street. But he used to be Di's cousin's dog before she rescued him and gave him to Nigel. So, he loved us. We were kind of his dog godparents. I kissed Di on the cheek and gave Zeus a scratch.

We sank into the couch together, red in hand. The TV was on but we weren't really watching.

'Well, that's great news about the apprenticeship! When do you start?' asked Di.

'I'm still not sure I want to.'

She turned from the TV to look at me. 'Why not?'

'Like we've spoken about, it's going to be less money.'

'We're comfortable enough, aren't we? We'll have enough.'

'Not if we have kids.'

'Are we going to have kids?'

'Aren't we?'

'Sure, but if we have kids we'll have to get married.'

'Let's get married then.'

That was it. I took her ring shopping the next day.

That year Sam's Island nearly burnt down. No one knows how it caught fire – lightning maybe. But he had no water to put it out. Luckily much of the structure on the island was built from rock, so the damage wasn't too bad. But it shook Old Sam. People from all over came to help him rebuild. HI even built a pipeline from Windy Ridge to the island so he'd have running water from then on.

On a clear, forecast to be forty-degree day, Harv called a stop-work meeting. He crammed all the shop stewards into one of the meeting rooms. It was tight. Odd that he hadn't dragged us to the mess.

Must be serious, I thought.

'There's been a reclaimer accident at Robe River. Snapped clean in half. Johnny was in the cabin.'

A few of the men gasped. I felt sick.

'He's dead,' said Harv.

Johnny was the steward with the safety concerns from our last union meeting. He had told us they were putting too much pressure on the reclaimer with the counterweights. He'd kept saying they were going to kill someone. They bloody killed him.

'That's murder,' said Tommy.

The blokes all nodded. We bowed our heads in a minute of silence for Johnny. And then we left. Alone in the cabin of the shiploader, my hands shook all over the controls.

I thought about Charlie and Susie. Something Charlie had said about getting married. I thought of Di and how she would be worried sick at the news of the horrific workplace death. And I thought I finally understood what Charlie had meant.

That I had never wanted to live more than when I wanted to live for someone else.

1988

In 1988, Ga sent me a scratchie for my birthday. I remember opening the card. I knew it was from her straightaway because the back flap of the envelope was tucked in, rather than licked and stamped on top. It was one of those watercolour kind of cards, with a red vintage car painted on the front and gold embossed words 'To my beautiful grandson' arching over it like a rainbow. Inside was her unmistakable octogenarian handwriting. All block letters.

DEAR GRANT,
HAPPY BIRTHDAY
LOVE GA X

Out of the card fell one of those crossword scratchies. The ones where you get a selection of letters at the bottom, and you scratch out the corresponding letters on the main board in the middle. Kind of like scrabble. However many words you completely scratched out would determine how much money you won. I won eight dollars.

I had just started my electrical apprenticeship in January. Signing the paperwork scared me. But Di was there, hand resting on my shoulder.

'We're looking at ten thousand dollars less than last year,' I said, waving my hand over the contract, my palm facing up to God.

She said what she always said to me. 'We'll work it out.'

That summer, the prisoners at Fremantle rioted. The inmates attacked guards with everything they could. Plates, buckets and mops. Food, the boiling water for the tea. Starting fires everywhere they went. They beat the guards and held them hostage for nineteen hours. Main Division went up in flames. The government had promised to decommission the place due to inhumane conditions five years earlier. A royal commission had recommended it. But nothing had been done. For some reason it got me thinking about Pope and his rogue, guerilla-style activism. The clock stolen from the Cott. The two-up on Anzac Day. What was all that for, if not for justice?

That feeling again – of pulling together, shared consciousness.

The Pilbara felt so familiar. The ancient landscape where a rich man flew his plane low enough to notice the rust colour of iron in the gorge and decided to make himself richer. The richness of this place has brought people from all over the world – each with their own agendas – to get richer and richer still. Iron ore mining built this state. And the boom pulled me in. My ticket out of prison. It was in the blood after all, mining. Ga's old man worked the coal trains as a trimmer – sorting the coal in the railway cars all the way from Walker's Pit to the River Tyne. Until 1922 when the coal seam ran out. They all got made redundant then. Would the iron ore ever run out here?

The death at Robe River. That feeling again.

It made me so fucking angry that these big companies cared more about their profit than the safety of their workers. That making money was more important than a worker making it home at the end of the day to greet their family. That they made money on Aboriginal land and felt no obligation to share this wealth with traditional owners. And that they barely paid any tax on that money because of successive pissant governments too scared to play hardball with the multinational big dogs.

But then you look at union guys like Harv. Unmoved by the money and power behind these companies. Unafraid to look them in straight in the eye and call them murderers if he has to. Since the Industrial Revolution – in coal country where Ga was born – unionists like Harv have given their lives to ensure workers have the right to get home safe. For the right to a weekend and adequate healthcare. For justice.

That feeling. Hope.

I've always found it strange how you don't consciously feel at home somewhere. It takes a while, right? When you move into a new place. And I've moved around more than most. It's just like: one day you're completely comfortable, and it feels like you've been there your whole life. I didn't know you could get that same feeling with people, until then.

Di fell pregnant in February. I don't remember us even trying, really. It happened quickly. We were happy. I kept trying to imagine what it was going to be like to be a father. I'd spend hours thinking about this future child, holding this baby without features. It didn't seem real.

Pippin was to marry in March. She'd be travelling to town from Kalgoorlie where she was working as a photographer. We'd already be in town for her wedding on the twelfth, so we organised our wedding for a week later, on the nineteenth, in order to save everyone on travel. Namely us. Pippin and Gary got married at the Fremantle Arts Centre. Di and I got married in her sister Marilyn's backyard in Carlisle. The reception was in Mum and Dave's backyard in Cottesloe, with the swimming pool all covered up for a makeshift dance floor. Scott, ever the comedian, was master of ceremonies at both weddings.

Sam and I went for a surf at Cott while I was down. Peter came along too. For old time's sake, we said. Out on the water, looking back at the foreshore and the Cott Hotel and the Ocean Beach Hotel, it didn't look like anything much had changed. Although everything felt a little smaller. I kept expecting the lifesavers to rock up on their yellow floaty boards and kick us out from the main break, but no one came.

We drove back up home to Dampier a month or so later. Di had to stop to piss at almost every servo along the way. When we got to Geraldton, we stopped for petrol.

'My old man lives here you know,' I said.

She looked blank.

'My biological father, I mean. Doug.'

'Where?'

'Geraldton. I don't know exactly. But I know Ga has the address.'

'You should get in touch with him.'

'I don't know if he'll want me to.'

'I'm sure he will. Tell him he's going to be a grandfather.'

'I don't know if I forgive him.'

'You don't have to.'

Di slept on the drive between Carnarvon and Pannawonica. The metro radio station had cut out, but I didn't bother tuning it to find the country channels. I sat in silence, listening to the slow breaths, in and out, that emanated from Di's sleep. Her hands were resting on her belly. The further north we drove, the bluer the sky looked. I had to jostle her awake after we'd pulled into the driveway and I'd finished getting the suitcases and boxes of gifts and miscellaneous crap inside.

I breathed in deeply – the country air, feeling lighter already than I had those few weeks in the city. There's nothing like a fifteen-hour drive to give you clarity.

I sat down at the kitchen bench and started writing a letter to the old man.

***

Cyclone Herbie hit the state out of nowhere. But it landed further south than we first thought. Carnarvon got hammered. It took out all the bananas, so the price of bananas went up. Everyone thought cyclone season was over. It felt strange to go on as normal – going to the shops and the pub and everything – while people's homes were being destroyed a few hundred kilometres down the coast. Kind of like when you see a homeless person on the street but you don't have any coins in your pocket. I felt a bit guilty.

Most people up north knew that I'd been inside. I'd told Di nearly straightaway. And she was so good about it. Sometimes the blokes would give me shit at footy or whatever. But a lot of them had been inside too. One day after training, one of the older blokes pulled me aside to tell me about his son. He'd gotten in a brawl at a party. No one was seriously hurt or anything, but the coppers caught him throwing a punch. And he'd been warned in the past. So he had to do a couple of months inside. The kid was only twenty.

'I was wondering if you could write a letter of support for him, Grant? Like, you've been inside, so you could say if you work hard you can pull yourself out of it. Be rehabilitated. Redeem yourself kind of thing.'

That's what it was. Redemption.

Towards the tail end of the footy season I ended up filling a spot in the A-grade side. As did Jacko. I started on the bench and Jacko was out on the ground, in the midfield. We were playing Wickham again. We were getting flogged. Maguire let me run out in the second quarter. Ducky was down in Perth, so Maguire was filling in. Maguire was different from Ducky in that he favoured a bit of analysis. Sort of a right-side-of-the-brain kind of bloke. So he was stressed. At half-time I was expecting a spray, but Maguire pulled us together in the huddle and spoke in a calm and measured fashion.

'Bullant, mate. You're getting killed in the back pocket. We need some height.'

Bullant nodded. Grudgingly.

'Grant, we'll move you into the backline. Bullant to the forward pocket.'

I looked at Bullant and he responded with a shrug. I hadn't played down the back since juniors. But I think we were all willing to give anything a try, being eleven and a half goals down.

And then the floodgates opened. Jacko roved it out of the middle, straight to Bullant, who converted it into a goal from the fifty-metre mark. Then Bullant took a contested mark inside fifty and converted it again. I punched it out of the square. And again. I rushed it behind. Jacko took a screamer right in the forward pocket and then kicked the goal. The guys in the middle were just peppering the forward fifty.

By three-quarter time we were only two goals behind. I could see Di in the stands with Jacko's partner, Wendy. Di's belly was protruding from under her jacket, green-and-gold scarf around her neck.

The last quarter was a battle. Jacko kicked a goal. Then Wickham returned serve. I'd punch it out, then their back man would flatten Bullant. The clock wound down. We were behind by seven. The ball was too far up the ground to score and Wickham had momentum. Then one of our midfielders took out the man on the run. The ball flew through the air, towards our forward fifty. Jacko scooped it up and kicked it from just outside the fifty-metre line. Goal. Siren. We won by a point. Maguire ran out onto the ground and grabbed the three of us in a headlock. Di and Wendy ran out onto the ground too. Di's voice was hoarse. Wendy was smiling.

'I deadset thought I was going to have the baby right there in the grandstand! I was clenching my arse so tight!' said Di.

Jacko got a few A-grade games after that. And Di and Wendy became inseparable.

As the due date drew nearer, I expected to feel different about the baby. Like I'd just settle in naturally to feeling like a father. But it didn't happen. And I wasn't so much anxious for the arrival, I just felt in the dark a bit. I had no idea what to expect. You didn't really find out the sex of the baby in those days, so we didn't even know that. It's an indescribable feeling, the period before becoming a father.

Since receiving my birthday card from Ga I'd been walking around with the eight-dollar winning scratchie in the back pocket of my stubbies. I had the afternoon off so I wandered over to the library to borrow a book. I decided on some true-crime thriller story. Then I popped into Woolies. And on the way back home I went by the newsagent.

'Hey mate, I've got a winner here,' I said, eight-dollar winning scratchie between my thumb and index finger.

'How big?' said the man.

'Not very.'

'Well, do you want to cash it in or swap it for a few more?'

Good question, I thought. They were all there under this plastic shield, on display. Brightly coloured. I definitely wanted to scratch again. That is how they get you.

'Yeah, okay I'll have eight dollars worth please.'

I handed it over and the man swapped me for three more, and I slipped them in the book.

I walked back home along the peninsula. Grey clouds were forming above the archipelago, threatening to build into a storm front and drift ashore. Sam's Island looked battered. Old Sam was still rebuilding from the fire. You could see the faint outline of the burnt-out shell of his summer garden facade.

Di was on the phone when I got home. I saw the look on her face as her eyes found mine. My legs crumbled beneath me.

I imagined Dave being called out there from the dispatch at Cottesloe Police Station. He would have been one of the first on the scene. The car parked at a plain little park in Churchlands. Exhaust pipe rammed through the crack in the window.

I imagined Pippin driving back from Kalgoorlie, for eight hours, not knowing what was coming but feeling it.

I imagined Jodee working at the pub, given instructions by management to go straight home.

I imagined Peta being pulled out of class and marched to the principal's office.

I imagined Mum.

Years earlier, I'd chosen to live.

When had Scott chosen to die?

The funeral was a blur. I really don't remember much of it. I don't even know if I read any poetry or hymns or whatever. Was he buried or cremated? I think he's buried, but I don't know. He's at Karrakatta, definitely. But I couldn't tell you where. We were all in shock, I suppose. Most of us still are.

Scott died on 6 October 1988. Two months to the day after his twenty-eighth birthday. Later we heard that he'd confessed his love to his best friend and housemate that day, and she'd rejected him. Whether or not that had anything to do with it, we didn't know – he didn't leave a note. Which I've wondered about, since. It didn't exactly seem like a spur of the moment kind of action. Somewhat premeditated. So I've wondered, selfishly, why no note? Could he not have left us with something? I know now, after experiencing many more deaths, that there is no such thing as closure. The sooner people realise that, the happier they'll be. Life is grotesque. People don't act in ways you expect them to. So holding out hope for closure, for some kind of logical explanation or meaning for everything, is simply a mug's game.

The more we thought about it, the more it became obvious that Scott probably had bipolar disorder. Whatever happiness we saw in him, the inverse must also have existed. In the shadows. We all loved him so much.

Our father was there, at the funeral and then the wake. It wasn't hard to recognise Doug. Di said it must have been like looking in a mirror. I told him about the letter. It hadn't arrived yet.

'Look at you,' he said, turning to Di. 'You're about to burst.'

'Feels like it,' she said, running her hands over her belly.

'When are you due?'

'Next month.'

'Do you know?' he let the question hang there without finishing the sentence.

'We don't know,' I said.

'But I know,' said Di, beaming. 'It's going to be a boy.'

We sank into the couch, even lower than usual given the extra weight. Di was past her due date now. We had the bag packed, ready to head straight to Nickol Bay Hospital as soon as it was time. I think I was more nervous about it all than Di was.

'As long as they give me the epidural,' was all she said.

I opened the book on the coffee table. I hadn't even started it yet, and it was probably already due back at the library. Slipped behind the cover page along with the library receipt were a couple of those crossword scratchies. I picked a coin out of my pocket and started to scratch. Nothing. The eight dollars had lulled me into a false sense of security. It was a patsy. I chucked it onto the coffee table.

'Pass us one,' said Di.

So I did. Plus the coin. I used my fingernails on the last one.

'Yes!' Di yelled out, waving the scratchie in front of me.

'How much?'

'Eight dollars!'

I laughed.

'What?' she asked.

'I've got ten thousand dollars here.'

'No way!' She grabbed the scratchie from my hand, studying it, before looking back up at me with tears in her eyes.

Within the hour Nigel was over, with Zeus, and a magnum of champagne. Then came Jacko and Wendy. And Tommy. And Peter. And Sam.

'Ten grand. Unbelievable,' said Peter, shaking his head.

'You're the luckiest man alive,' said Sam, with a wink, knowing damn well that I wasn't.

Tommy slapped me on the back. 'Don't know what you were worried about,' he said, topping up my glass of champagne. 'It looks like your apprenticeship's already paid for itself!'

That night I dreamed about the baby. One of those dreams where the image isn't complete in your head, so you can't actually see anything, but you know that they're there. She made me feel like I was vast, that this was the beginning of the great story of us. My daughter and I.

PENANG PRISON

The hardest thing to get used to was the humidity. It just felt like shit being sweaty all the time. The days were so slow and with nothing else to focus on, all you could think about was the humidity. If it were a dry heat, he could probably handle it, Charlie thought. But the humidity – it just gets to you. Especially with all the other sweaty blokes crammed in there. It didn't feel like death row to Charlie. It was too mundane.

Charlie got along with the guards alright. One of them knew his contact in Kuala Lumpur, so he'd been slipping Charlie dope for the past couple of months. Another one knew a guy who knew the lead prosecutor in the trial. Apparently they were terrified of an appeal because the cops had mishandled the evidence or something. And they knew it'd knock over their conviction. Charlie was buoyed by this information.

And he trusted that the Australian Government would be able to sort something out with the Malaysians, if not for him then to at least save face. The Yanks were all over it too. His mum had sent him clippings from the *New York Times*.

Kevin wouldn't shut the fuck up about his groin injury. Charlie had tried to reason with him – the more he groaned, the more it pissed off the guards, who in turn kicked the shit out of his groin again. It was a vicious, never-ending cycle. But he wouldn't listen. He'd cry and groan all night, calling out for his mother. Unfortunately, you can't fix stupid, thought Charlie.

For Charlie, time not thinking about the humidity was spent reading books. He read a lot – whatever he could find. Sometimes it was something new. Or it was something he'd read what felt like a million times before. Like *The Catcher in the Rye*. Sometimes he got so deep in reading he forgot where he was. Or was that the dope? thought Charlie.

Charlie didn't receive as much mail as Kevin did. Every other day Kevin seemed to receive something. He'd wail out at whoever's name was on the back of the envelope and tear it open, reading it and blubbering all over it, then clutching it to his chest. Charlie's mum would write to him sometimes. Mostly with newspaper clippings and a bit of news about his family. And she'd write anytime the prime minister said anything publicly about the case.

Every couple of days Charlie's lawyer would visit. So would Kevin's. It would always wind Kevin up, for some reason, Charlie noticed. He'd start mouthing off into the abyss, screaming about the appeals process and the rule of law and whatever else. Charlie tried to block it out. He was well beyond the fury he had first felt when Kevin blew their cover at the airport. But it simmered beneath him still, and he couldn't help but think about all the different choices he had made in his haste to get there that could have engineered a different outcome. When his rage simmered to the top, after some intense ruminating, he'd scream back at Kevin. But it happened rarely. Charlie just kept on reading, slowly passing the days.

At some point Charlie noticed that Kevin had started to decline. He had a strange energy about him. He was morose. In contrast to his wailing before, it was unsettling behaviour. It unsettled the guards too, in a different way from Charlie. They took Kevin's silence as determination, and suspected him of plotting an escape. But Charlie knew he was too stupid for that. One afternoon the sun was streaming through the barred window, and it pierced through the room and left a shard of light on Kevin's face. Charlie could see he'd given up.

There was a line in *The Catcher in the Rye* that stuck in his brain. But it wasn't a line exactly, it was more of an image.

The eponymous image. A boy on the edge of a cliff. Charlie felt big. Vast. And he couldn't shake it. It took days for him to realise it reminded him of Susie. When he did, he felt his face prickle and flush. He didn't think about her much anymore. In fact, he couldn't remember the last time he did. But then there she was, in him. A phantom pain in a missing limb.

Even when the guards moved them on to the anteroom beside the gallows, Charlie thought they had a chance. He pictured his mum and his lawyer, with the Feds, poring over the detail of the latest appeal with the prosecutor. He pictured the media scrum waiting to interview him upon his release. He pictured himself on the Triumph Bonneville Silver Jubilee. He pictured the boy on the edge of the cliff.

FAST FORWARD

Dad orders the bruschetta and a mid-strength beer. The wooden tables are wiped clean but feel sticky, a by-product of years of use. We're at my local – an eclectic mix of rustic and kitsch decor, food stuffs on open shelves, fake creeper plants and exposed brick. Wine glasses frame the bar like a halo. Fresh bombolini and pastries look like fake displays in glass boxes. Little crosses made from sticky tape mark the floor, denoting where to stand. We sign in via a QR code but we're not yet wearing masks. I order poached eggs on multigrain – the crunchy Italian bread with sharp edges – an almond latte and an Aperol Spritz.

We're in the corner by the window, which looks out onto the deep orange and royal blue of Beaufort Street. There's the faint sound of cars passing on the strip. Instructions in the kitchen. The clink of cutlery against plates. I prop up my phone up the table against the little brown pot housing the sugar sachets, and when our plates are cleared away, I start recording again.

Our economy is booming while governments around the world are effectively printing money to survive. Not too long ago, mineworkers made redundant in WA found work as Uber drivers and you couldn't find a young person willing to risk an engineering degree. Now the industry is crying out for workers. Such is the cyclical nature of the beast. Dad's still a mineworker. But he can see the writing on the wall. Rio Tinto's destruction of Juukan Gorge – the 46,000-year-old rock shelter of immense cultural significance to our First Nations Australians – has cast a shadow over the entire industry. This watershed event has rightly shone a forensic light on the way in which mining companies interact with local Indigenous stakeholders. The pandemic has shut our country's borders, exacerbating the skills shortage. And climate change risks the business model of all extractive industries – because whether or not they develop fossil fuels, for now they are powered by them.

Dad says he was never the same after his mum left. I don't know if he means when she left him at Ga's when he was six or left him boarding in Cottesloe at fifteen. I don't ask.

He just went kind of funny, he says.

He knows rationally that she needed to work. That it can't have been easy for her, getting divorced in the 1960s in a city which was – and still is – effectively a country town. But what is rationality to an abandoned child?

I tell him I understand. I feel it too. Even though Mum's body failed her after being sick for half of my life. That it was the non-Hodgkin's lymphoma and hardly her choice to die. But I was only nine. And I didn't get to see her at the hospital. She didn't leave a note – nothing to steer me into womanhood. Just a teddy bear and the weight of the world on my shoulders. I was abandoned too.

It's not blame, it just is.

Joss, my grandmother, stayed with us after Mum died. In the front room. She still tells me about how I woke her up, sleepwalking into her room in the middle of the night. She thought I was a ghost. She helped me pick out a bright pink outfit for the funeral. And she was the first to buy me tampons and sanitary pads. She was there, and I love her for that. Like Ga with Dad. And Pippin and Scott. Ga, my namesake. Maybe the maternal instinct skips a generation in our family – a recessive gene. Maybe it's every family if you look hard enough.

Or maybe there are no patterns and simply coincidences.

It's a coincidence that we're in Mount Lawley, where Charlie was born in the same year as Dad. Dad says again that he could have saved Charlie's life if he'd ratted on him when he went down. Maybe that's true. But I think it's survivor's guilt. That their lives started out much the same. And how Dad can count on two hands the number of people he knew who died from a heroin overdose. That it could have been him. And there's no reason that it wasn't.

For Scott – I like to think of him as my own brother, who keeps his cards close to his chest while Dad and I pour our hearts out all over the table. Simply, he is missed. Some things are too painful.

I'm thinking about work tomorrow. I work in politics, like my brother does. We inherited empathy and a social conscience from the Old Boy. And through a lifetime's worth of discussing industrial relations, unionism and fairness – a deep understanding that there is hope in collectivism and purpose in public service. Tomorrow I'll fly up to the Pilbara again, this time to see the Port of Dampier and the North West Shelf – powering our economy – where our parents were working when they first met.

And I'm thinking that I write because Dad taught me how to read before I went to school. Back when Dad was home and Mum worked, before she got sick. That right now, in this country, school is not enough. It should be. Because the world will continue to change, and more and more people will need to use their brains more than their bodies to work and live. For now, for me, I know I'm lucky.

And I'm grateful – that I am who I am in spite of him and because of him.

AUTHOR'S NOTES

One of my favourite elements of my dad's story is the setting. I love his stark recollections of place and his connection to the iconic geography and culture of Perth – our home. My research inevitably led me to delve into the broader history of this place. What struck me is the common thread of imprisonment and injustice upon which Western Australia is built. I provide that background here in the hope that it will help the reader understand that Dad's story is just one part of something much bigger.

Wadjemup

During the Ice Age, Wadjemup was connected to the mainland of Western Australia. The Whadjuk people of the Noongar nation would walk there for important meetings and ceremonies. When the ice melted, the sea levels rose, forming the island Wadjemup, alongside Ngooloomayup and Meandup. No longer able to walk there, Noongar people knew Wadjemup to be a place of transition between the physical and spiritual worlds.

Under the guise of the *Aborigines Protection Act 1886*, the Indigenous peoples of Western Australia were enslaved. Men were forced into harsh labour – farming, mining, construction. Women and children were forced into domestic servitude, much like African slaves in Europe and the United States of America. Land was stolen. The colonials cleared everything away, depleting the vegetation and hunting fare that Indigenous peoples relied upon to eat.

If an Indigenous person refused forced labour, or contested their land being stolen, or hunted introduced animals for feed, they were imprisoned. The Roundhouse prison on the mainland soon became overwhelmed, so the colonials sent Indigenous peoples over to Wadjemup with chains around their necks. They called it by its foreign name: Rottnest Island. European sailors had observed it hundreds of years earlier, while sailing to Indonesia, chasing spices, slaves and shipwrecks. The Dutch eventually called it *'t Eylandt Rottenest* – Rats' Nest Island. Because they thought the quokkas were giant rats.

There at Wadjemup, the place where the spirits are, the Aboriginal prisoners were forced to quarry limestone to build their own prison – the Quod. The cells were around two by one-and-a-half metres – the size of an average queen-sized bed. And they housed up to seven prisoners each. Cells had no fireplaces or windows, so there was no reprieve from the weather. They had no beds so the prisoners slept on the dirt. They had no toilets, nor even buckets, so the prisoners went where they slept.

Prisoners endured lashings and beatings. They worked in extreme heat on construction projects for the colonials. They built the lighthouses. They slept chained together at night. Any undisciplined prisoners were killed – hanged or shot.

As the prison population continued to grow, the Quod became overcrowded, exacerbating the spread of disease. In the tiny, windowless cells, disease took hold. The Europeans had brought colds, flu, dysentery, measles – and each disease spread through the prison like a bushfire. Winter was particularly bad. Many more died.

When the prison was finally closed, nearly one hundred years after it opened, Aboriginal prisoners continued in slavery for another thirty years, building roads and other infrastructure for the newly reinvented holiday island. The existing prison infrastructure was repurposed for recreational facilities. And the Quod was converted to tourist accommodation. From 1838 to 1904, nearly four thousand Aboriginal people were imprisoned on Rottnest Island. From 1904 to 1931 they were enslaved there. At least 370 prisoners died – Australia's largest incidence of deaths in custody – at the Quod. Where people from the mainland continued to stay and party until the commercial lease finally expired in 2018.

Fremantle Prison

Like the Roundhouse and the Quod before it, Fremantle Prison – originally, 'The Convict Establishment' – was built by convict labour and limestone quarried onsite. British convicts in the thousands levelled the hill and used the limestone spoils to build the main cell block – a big rectangular hall-like structure. Four storeys of cells lined the walls with an open-air area in the middle obstructed only by several layers of suicide net. On each corner of the heavy limestone walls sat a rifleman in a gun tower. Fremantle Prison opened after construction of the main cell block was complete in 1855. From 1886 until its demise over a century later, it was Western Australia's maximum-security prison.

The worst criminals in Western Australian history were imprisoned or hanged at Fremantle Prison.

The last man hanged there was Eric Edgar Cooke. Also known as The Night Caller, Cooke killed eight people and assaulted many more between 1959 and 1963. In his testimony he recounted playing with his children in the morning before a murder spree. His killings were so random that it wasn't until he confessed that the police linked the cases. He shot and strangled men and women. He ran people over with his car. He said he felt like God. He spent 333 days in Fremantle Prison before they sent him to the gallows.

His body, alongside others collected by the hangman, are buried in unmarked graves on the grounds between New Division and Main Parade Ground within the prison confines.

By the 1960s the prison was severely overcrowded. Rats and cockroaches infested the soft limestone. There was no heating, cooling or even insulation in the buildings. Prisoners found maggots in their food. They were afforded only two showers per week, so a dank stench of body odour permeated the main cell block at all times. Despite it being clear in the 1960s that Fremantle Prison was not fit for purpose, successive governments deferred calls to relocate the prisoners to a new facility. As is common in politics, with the perpetual factors of the budget bottom line and short electoral cycles, big correction reforms were a can kicked down the road.

In 1973 the state of Western Australia launched a royal commission into incidents of violence at Fremantle Prison. Director of the Department of Corrections at the time, Mr Colin Campbell, described Fremantle Prison as ‘archaic’, and argued that the prison was ‘so old and cramped’ that it would be ‘impossible to extend or improve facilities to allow for meaningful recreation for inmates’. Mr Campbell stated then that government was limited in what it could do to improve the lives of inmates at Fremantle and that a replacement facility must be found. Further, he found systemic issues with administration and that the ancient confinement cells, known as the ‘chokey’, were not suitable to hold inmates except in an emergency and should be discontinued. ‘I don’t know of a worse prison in the world,’ said Mr Campbell.

By the 1980s Fremantle Prison was uninhabitable. The

summer heat on the corrugated-iron roof would heat the top floor cells up to fifty degrees Celsius. It was still over capacity. They were still using buckets as toilets. The gallows facilitated state-sanctioned killings until the death penalty was outlawed in 1984. In 1986 the Western Australian State Cabinet resolved to finally shut Fremantle Prison down, developing plans for a new maximum-security prison at Casuarina.

By 1988 the prisoners were ropable. The prison was a tinderbox yearning for a spark. On the fourth and fifth of January they rioted, set to burn the place down. It was reportedly a forty-degree day. At first unlock there was a dispute between a prisoner and an officer. Smith, the prisoner, was late out of his cell and reportedly became abusive when hurried along by the officer. The 'upset' and 'hostile' prisoner was restrained and hauled into an observation cell. Later in the day, Smith was released into the yard with the other prisoners. He sported marks over his neck and face, and the prisoners considered the incident as a bashing. The officer in question had been known to be a violent prick in the past. The prisoners collated a list of demands, including an audience with the superintendent, but were refused.

By lunchtime the officers had agreed to take Smith to the prison hospital to be examined. The prisoners were empowered. To settle the growing tension, the superintendent decided to allow the prisoners free time in the afternoon, rather than sending them to work. This allowed the prisoners to continue their plotting. They held a series of meetings to discuss their plans. Tension and resentment were building. An officer passed a charge sheet through to Smith in the yard, which he tore up in response, to rapturous cheering and jeering from the other inmates. The officers couldn't decide how to respond. By three forty pm, after counting the number of officers stationed at Main Division, the prisoners had decided to riot.

On the call for meals, the prisoners rushed the grill gate and stormed Main Division. They attacked officers with plates, makeshift weapons and boiling water, and then stole their keys. They lit fires in the cells that licked up the walls and took hold on the jarrah beams of the roof. Officers were in varying states of control and retreat with the rioters. When the fire spread, prisoners rushed to save their belongings from the cells. The rioters took officers as hostage for collateral against any more brutality. They asked for nothing in return for the hostages but for a meeting with the executive director, no physical reprisals, and baked beans and cigarettes. The siege lasted nineteen hours. Fifteen officers were injured. One suffered severe burns to forty-five per cent of his body. It cost nearly two million dollars in damage at the time. Thirty-three prisoners were charged and tried.

The subsequent inquiry found discontent at the state of the prison, and the widespread brutality perpetrated by the officers, was such that the riot was pretty much inevitable. The inquiry described the conditions at Fremantle Prison as 'substandard' and 'early Victorian', with prisoners 'compelled to eat, sleep and defecate in the one small and confined space', one which was infested with cockroaches and 'plague of mice'. Short-term, minimum-security prisoners were mixing with hardened murderers and psychopaths. Fremantle Prison was the only prison in the state that served the 'psychiatrically disturbed'. Officers were punitive and abusive. Administrative failures had led to gross negligence. In the week before the riot, another prisoner had approached an officer about appealing his transfer to a prison in Albany. No appeal was lodged or actioned. Without administrative recourse, the prisoner slashed his wrists in order to stay.

Among the inquiry's recommendations were eradicating the 'plague of cockroaches and insects'; installing working, sewered toilets in Main Division; considering a 'system of forced air, or other form of ventilation to the cells'; a later lock-up during the 'height of summer' to 'allow cells to cool'; ending the requirement for prisoners to wear communal underwear; and prohibiting officers' use of 'disparaging language' to prisoners.

In 1990 the Fremantle Prison Conservation and Future Use project handed down its report to the Western Australian Government and recommended that the prison be conserved as a significant cultural heritage site. The WA Government accepted the recommendation, and the last prisoners were transferred to Casuarina Prison in 1991.

Brian Geoffrey Chambers

Australia's relationship with heroin really kicked off during the Vietnam War. Not only did diggers experiment with drugs while on deployment, but US servicemen on R&R on the East Coast also brought heroin and other drugs into the country, introducing it first into the red-light districts of Sydney and Melbourne. The heroin trade grew from there, disseminating through the suburbs throughout the 1960s, and making its way to the West. In the early 1970s, the US Government directed the Green Berets and the CIA to buy opium directly from growers – who were moonlighting as guerillas – in exchange for loyalty from the rebel regime in Vietnam. State-sanctioned heroin.

By the end of the war, Australia had a smack habit.

Crime was rampant in Perth after the Vietnam War. The casino in Burswood wasn't to be built until the 1980s, so gambling – and subsequently drug distribution – was facilitated through organised crime. Punters would frequent illegal clubs based in Northbridge and Fremantle. And drug dealers would utilise the premises for their own exploits. Such was the business model of Paolo Musarri – a slick, Sicilian-born criminal with a gambling addiction and a stolen-car racket based out of a panelbeater's in O'Connor. The bloke hated the banks and kept his profits under his mattress.

Perth was the perfect heroin hub in the 1970s. Closer to South-East Asia than to the East Coast, the sleepy town had an underdeveloped and negligibly resourced drug squad, which meant there was little to no patrol at Fremantle Port. And the product from South-East Asia was of the highest quality in the world. Drug smugglers were walking the stock right off the dock and sending the raw product to Sydney, from where it would be distributed across the country. Police and the media were oblivious. Until the late 1970s, the heroin distribution network in Perth – then at a nascent stage – consisted of sparsely located, small-time dealers. That was until the Italian syndicate staked its claim on the heroin market. Italian players had been raising capital by cultivating marijuana in the South-West. Money was laundered through pizza bars, nightclubs, building companies and car yards. The syndicate grew and subsequently invested in heroin – transporting it from Sydney across the Nullarbor and distributing it out of subsidiaries in Perth, Fremantle, Bentley and Balcatta. Two years later the Italians were importing the heroin product to Perth directly from South-East Asia.

Paul Musarri was essentially a middleman for the Italians. He and around ten others were running the Perth street trade by the early 1980s, with Musarri overseeing the Fremantle cell. He would recruit and pay mules to transport heroin into Perth from Sydney first, and then South-East Asia, on behalf of his investors. Musarri would front the cash – let's say ten thousand dollars – and a mule would pick up five kilograms of heroin from Malaysia and bring it to Perth on their person. The final sum – $20,000 – would then change hands upon safe entry of the product. Everything from the point of recruitment and the planning of trips to the exchange of goods and sale would take place over a meal at an Italian restaurant in Bicton, with the funds laundered through its books. One of Musarri's favourite, most trusted mules was Brian Geoffrey Chambers.

Chambers was born on 30 April 1957 in Mount Lawley. His parents, country folk from the Wheatbelt, travelled around the country in the earthmoving business, before settling in Bicton – where Chambers and his siblings went to school. Chambers was an introvert. Funny and highly intelligent – with IQ bordering on gifted – he loved science and sought a career in science at a young age. But like many other kids of that era, Chambers fell into drugs – marijuana at first and heroin by the age of fifteen. He started breaking into homes in Bicton and engaging in low-level dealing to fund his drug habit, dropping out halfway through his fourth year of high school. Chambers worked with his dad, fixing ceilings, before leaving for Darwin in 1977.

There Chambers met Dang, his first love. Through her contacts in Thailand, Chambers began trafficking Thai heroin throughout the country. It was arguably the best grade of heroin in Australia at the time. Responsible for a series of burglaries in the Northern Territory, Chambers and Dang moved to New South Wales and began building a heroin empire in Kings Cross – dealing directly out of Chambers' MG sports car. Perhaps seeking to settle down, the couple shortly moved back to Chambers' hometown of Perth in 1978.

Eventually their chickens came home to roost. Chambers

and Dang were arrested on the Cappuccino Strip in Fremantle in 1979. It was around this time that Chambers had started working for Musarri, running heroin from the East Coast back to Perth. Chambers was acquitted, but Dang was deported back to Thailand. Chambers, heartbroken, left town again.

Chambers met nursing student Sue Jacobsen in Sydney. By 1980 they were back in Perth, living in the house of Chambers' aunt in Cottesloe, and it wasn't long before Sue developed a heroin habit to match Chambers'. That same year she accompanied him on their first international drug run to Nepal, smuggling 170 grams of heroin back to Perth in her vagina.

From 1981 to 1983 Chambers made at least twelve international drug-smuggling trips – mostly to Malaysia – with Sue and with other mules. He was notorious in the underworld around the country for his sleek ability to import the highest grades of heroin and avoid suspicion from customs officers. Everyone wanted a piece of him. He had links to the top of the chain of the Italian syndicate, meeting regularly with elite crime bosses with direct familial ties to the Mafia. And he boasted powerful contacts in heroin-producing cities like Penang.

Chambers favoured the 'half up, half down' method of drug smuggling in which he would crush the heroin – the pink-and-brown crystallised rocks – into powder, and compact it into empty plastic thirty-five-millimetre film containers. He'd then slice open the plastic, remove the compact brick of powder and wrap the brick in a condom. Well, double-wrap actually, just in case. He could fit three of the twice-wrapped bricks in his anal passage, having emptied his bowels via laxatives in preparation. Any surplus bricks would be swallowed. He could carry half a kilogram of heroin in his body and subsequently evacuate the goods upon arrival at home port. Body searches were uncommon in Australia at the time, so it proved to be a fruitful method.

Although it's impossible to accurately quantify, it's estimated that Chambers imported twenty million dollars worth of heroin during this time. Throughout this period, he maintained strong relationships with his clientele in Perth, a tight group of dealers, addicts and friends who only ever knew him by his work alias, 'Charlie'.

Charlie and Sue were eventually caught in Singapore. Charlie had a stash for personal use in his pocket and got frisked at the airport. But he bought his way out. Lucky, given Singapore had the death penalty for drug trafficking at the time. Upon returning to Cottesloe, Charlie and Sue were robbed at gunpoint at their home. Spooked, they swapped their sports car for a four-wheel drive and fled the state. And on 15 May 1983, near Penong, South Australia, they wrote the car off. Charlie was driving, stoned. He rolled the car and Sue was thrown from the vehicle. Upon inspection, the cops found a kilogram of cannabis in the side door. Sue spent five days in a coma before she died. On

20 May, Sue Jacobsen's death notice in *The West* read: *Dearly loved, constant and loving companion of Geoffrey. Till we meet again.* And such was Charlie's state of mind that he asked South Australian police for his bag of pot back.

After Sue's death, Charlie was gaunt, pale and a slave to his smack habit. Some said he had a death wish. By July he was back in Malaysia, facilitating a heroin run for Musarri. Not the mule this time, Charlie was brokering a deal between Musarri's runners from Perth and a contact in Penang. Musarri, intent on maximising his cut, instructed Charlie to steal some heroin from the larger stash, to be retrieved at a later date. So Charlie did, and buried the package under a palm tree on Batu Ferringhi Beach. Musarri's runners were then caught in Perth, but nobody talked. And Charlie walked free.

Charlie was broke and desperate to head back to Penang to retrieve the buried heroin. Musarri was struggling to raise the capital for the trip. He was mad too, because he'd already given Charlie five thousand dollars one month earlier, and Charlie had blown it – he said he'd been busted on a dodgy passport and had to pay his way out, but Musarri wasn't buying it. Regardless, they both wanted the package retrieved.

Charlie took a sabbatical down south with some friends. By the time he returned to Perth, Musarri – through his associate John Asiack – had recruited a new mule: Kevin Barlow, a young man boarding at his girlfriend's flat. Charlie checked out Barlow at the Italian restaurant in Bicton and the trip was a go. And two months after burying the stash, Charlie was back at Bato Ferringhi Beach digging it up.

The pair set off on 28 October 1983, Charlie from Sydney and Barlow from Perth. Although initially advised to stay at separate hotels, they ended up sharing a room in Kuala Lumpur first, and then Penang. Upon the return, Barlow got cold feet and refused to do the 'half up, half down' method. Charlie relented, and let Barlow instead carry the stash in a suitcase. But when they got to the airport, Barlow was sweating profusely and shaking uncontrollably. Whether Barlow caught the attention of authorities or whether they'd been tipped off in the first place is still unknown. But the men were apprehended at Penang International Airport on 9 November 1983. Barlow had around 180 grams of pure heroin in the bag. More than ten times the limit of fifteen grams, which carried a mandatory death sentence under the country's new narcotics law passed that year. They were charged with drug trafficking and sent to Penang Prison to await trial.

Charlie and Barlow were locked in a two-by-three metre cell with three other men for twenty-two hours a day. No radio. No TV. No exercise. Charlie got on well with other prisoners and read a lot. But Barlow's health deteriorated and he was often distressed. They both continued using heroin. Both men's legal teams blamed the other. Neither expected a guilty verdict. On 1 August 1985 they were convicted and sentenced to death.

They appealed to the Supreme Court of Malaysia countless

times for clemency but were rejected. They pushed ahead to execution without all the pleas being heard, against United Nations doctrine, as put to authorities by Amnesty International. Prime Minister Bob Hawke, along with Britain's Margaret Thatcher, appealed for mercy but all appeals and calls for a stay of execution failed.

The men were hanged side by side at dawn on 7 July 1986. Hawke called it 'barbaric'.

John Asciak was convicted of conspiring with Chambers and Barlow to import the heroin into Australia. Although Paul Musarri has since been charged for other heroin trafficking offences – he was one of the first principal Perth drug dealers charged with a major drug offence – he was never tried in the Barlow–Chambers affair. Nor was anyone else higher up the chain of the Fremantle cell or the broader Italian syndicate.

Supposedly, an associate of Asiack's – Gerry Maio – was aggrieved about being refused a cut in the deal, so he had tipped off the Perth drug squad. Other reports suggest Barlow's landlady told her brother-in-law, who alerted a Perth detective, who then took his concerns to the Australian Federal Police.

Regardless of who knew what before the apprehension, what is known is that Barlow confessed to an Australian Federal Police officer immediately after his arrest. He identified senior members of the Italian syndicate. But it took years for the freshly instated National Crime Authority (today's Australian

Criminal Intelligence Commission [ACIC]) to make arrests, or for subsequent prosecutions to eventuate. Without this delay, such prosecutions may have provided leverage for Australia to get Chambers and Barlow back home for trial or, at the very least, saved their lives.

'Lambs to the slaughter' was how one investigator described them.

REFERENCES

Grant's story

Oral histories recorded with interviewee Grant Tree and the author via iPhone Voice Memos:

15 February 2020, Warnbro, WA

11 March 2020, Mount Lawley, WA

3 May 2020, Warnbro, WA

18 July 2020, Mount Lawley, WA

Archival *West Australian* print newspaper articles provided to the author by John Arthur.

Barry, Paul. *The Rise and Fall of Alan Bond*. Penguin, 1991.

Ellem, Bradon. 'Contested communities: geo-histories of unionism', *Journal of Organizational Change Management,* 21:4(2008): 433–450. doi.org/10.1108/09534810810884830.

Kennedy, Peter. *Tales from Boomtown: Western Australian Premiers From Brand to Barnett.* UWA Publishing, 2014.

Murujuga Aboriginal Corporation. 'About: Language Groups', 2021, murujuga.org.au/about/language-groups.

'National strike grips Australia', *The New York Times,* 13 July 1976, nytimes.com/1976/07/13/archives/national-strike-grips-australia-unions-in-24hour-walkout-over.html.

Salinger, J.D. *The Catcher in the Rye*. Penguin, 1945.

Sheen, Robyn L. 'Patterns in Australian Industrial Conflict: 1973–1989', PhD dissertation. Australian National University, 1992.

State of Western Australia. 'Tree, Grant Fremantle Prison Prisoner Card', 1981. Department of Corrections Archive. Accessed via Western Australia State Library, 2021.

Taylor, G.M. *Georgina May*. Self-published, 1996.

Wadjemup

Martin, Wayne. Address to 35th Annual Australia and New Zealand Law and History Society Conference, 'Aboriginal People at the Periphery'. Supreme Court of Western Australia, 2016, supremecourt.wa.gov.au/_files/35th_Annual_Australia_and_New_Zealand_Law_and_History_Society_Conference_Martin_CJ_5_Dec_2016.pdf

McGlade, Hannah. 'Rottnest Island "tent land" closure an important day for Aboriginal people', *ABC News*, 31 May 2018, abc.net.au/news/2018-05-31/quod-rottnest-island-aboriginal-land-mass-burial-gravesite/9811930.

Melville, Kirsti. 'Rottnest Island: Black prison to white playground.' *ABC News*, 16 October, 2016, abc.net.au/news/2016-10-25/rottnest-island-black-prison-to-white-playground/7962940.

Rottnest Island Authority, 'Aboriginal Culture and History of Wadjemup/Rottnest Island', 2021, rottnestisland.com/the-island/about-the-island/ourhistory/aboriginal-history.

'Waking up to Wadjemup', Office of the Registrar of Indigenous Corporations, n.d., oric.gov.au/publications/spotlight/waking-wadjemup.

Fremantle Prison

Acott, Kent. 'How a riot brought about the demise of Fremantle Prison 30 years ago and how it's incorporated in new tours', *The West Australian*, 19 February 2018, thewest.com.au/news/wa/how-a-riot-brought-the-demise-of-fremantle-prison-30-years-ago-and-how-its-incorporated-in-new-tours-ng-b88744427z.

Clarke, Tim. 'Cooke's final walk still echoes', *The West Australian*, 26 October, 2014, thewest.com.au/news/wa/cookes-final-walk-still-echoes-ng-ya-379777.

Commonwealth of Australia. 'Report of the Inquiry into the Death of Robert Joseph Walker', Royal Commission into Aboriginal Deaths in Custody, 27 February 1991, nla.gov.au/nla.obj-1940944447.

Fremantle Prison: The Convict Establishment. 'A Brief History', fremantleprison.com.au/history-heritage/history/a-brief-history.

Haebich, Anna. 'Revisiting the trial of Martha Rendell', *The New Critic,* 13:1–14, December 2010, ias.uwa.edu.au/new-critic/thirteen/haebich.

Office of the Inspector of Custodial Services. 'Report of the Enquiry into the Causes of the Riot, Fire and Hostage Taking at Fremantle Prison on the 4th and 5th of January 1988', 17 February 1988, oics.wa.gov.au/wp-content/uploads/2013/12/Fremantle_prison_riot_inquiry_19881.pdf.

State of Western Australia. 'Report of the Royal Commission upon Various Allegations of Assault on or Brutality to Prisoners in Fremantle Prison', 14 March 1973, parliament.wa.gov.au/intranet/libpages.nsf/WebFiles/RC+1973/$FILE/0002116.pdf.

State of Western Australia. 'Regional Report of Inquiry into Underlying Issues in Western Australia. Royal Commission into Aboriginal Deaths in Custody', Commonwealth of Western Australia, 1991, parlinfo.aph.gov.au/parlInfo/download/publications/tabledpapers/HPP032016008902/upload_pdf/HPP032016008902.pdf.

Stewart, Tracey. Serial killer Eric Edgar Cooke's voice heard 53 years after his execution', *ABC News*, 4 December 2019, abc.net.au/news/2017-11-14/eric-edgar-cooke-serial-killer-voice-heard-53-years-later/9122724.

Caporn, Dylan. 'Cabinet papers revisited: Plain sailing for Brian Burke but pressure on for America's Cup party', *The West Australian*, 10 June 2017, thewest.com.au/news/wa/cabinet-papers-revisited-plain-sailing-for-brian-burke-but-pressure-on-for-americas-cup-party-ng-b88500105z.

Brian Geoffrey Chambers

Adshead, Gary & Cowan, Sean. 'Perth's dark underbelly', *The West Australian*, 24 May 2010, thewest.com.au/news/australia/perths-dark-underbelly-ng-ya-211420.

Bull, Melissa. *Governing the Heroin Trade: From Treaties to Treatment (Law Ethics and Governance)*. Taylor & Francis Ltd, 2008.

Clarke, Tim. 'Barlow and Chambers, heroin and the underworld: Paul Musarri's life of crime', *The West Australian*, 7 September 2016, thewest.com.au/news/wa/barlow-and-chambers-heroin-and-the-underworld-paul-musarris-life-of-crime-ng-ya-117585.

Crossette, Barbara. 'Hangings prompt bitter reactions', *The New York Times*, 8 July 1986, nytimes.com/1986/07/08/world/hangings-prompt-bitter-reactions.html.

Dadah is Death/A Long Way From Home. London, Jerry (dir), Home Productions, Roadshow Coote & Carroll, Samuel Goldwyn Television, Steve Krantz Productions, 1988.

Hall, Wayne and Degenhardt, Louisa. 'The Australian Illicit Drug Reporting System: Monitoring trends in illicit drug availability, use and drug-related harm in Australia 1996–2006', *Contemporary Drug Problems* 36(3–4): 643–661; 377–378, journals.sagepub.com/doi/abs/10.1177/009145090903600317.

Hiett, Peter. 'Brian Chambers and Kevin Barlow executed in Malaysia', *The Guardian*, 8 July 1986, theguardian.com/theguardian/1986/jul/07/fromthearchive.

Silvester, John. 'Dancing with death – politics, power and the death penalty vie with hypocrisy', *The Age*, 19 February 2015, theage.com.au/national/victoria/dancing-with-death--politics-power-and-the-death-penalty-vie-with-hypocrisy-20150219-13iziy.html.

Williams, David. *This Little Piggy Stayed Home: Barlow, Chambers and the Mafia*. Panorama Books, 1989.

First published 2023 by
FREMANTLE PRESS

Fremantle Press Inc. trading as Fremantle Press
PO Box 158, North Fremantle, Western Australia, 6159
fremantlepress.com.au

Cover image courtesy of Jo and Dave Tree.
Designed by Nada Backovic, nadabackovic.com.
Printed and bound in Australia by Griffin Press.

ISBN 9781760991883 (paperback)
ISBN 9781760991890 (ebook)

Fremantle Press is supported by the State Government through the Department of Local Government, Sport and Cultural Industries.

Fremantle Press respectfully acknowledges the Wadjak people of the Noongar nation as the traditional owners and custodians of the land where we work in Walyalap.